-2

THE FOURTH CUP

THE
FOURTH
CUP

Unveiling the Mystery
of the Last Supper
and the Cross

Scott Hahn

Foreword by Brant Pitre

IMAGE
New York

Library of Congress Cataloging-in-Publication Data is
available upon request

ISBN 978-1-5247-5879-0
Ebook ISBN 978-1-5247-5880-6

Printed in the United States of America

Jacket design by Jess Morphew
Jacket image: The Agony in the Garden *(oil on canvas),*
Giordano Luca (1634–1705)/Hospital Tavera, Toledo, Spain/
Bridgeman Image

10 9 8 7 6 5 4 3 2 1

First Edition

To Marcus Grodi,

dear friend, fellow pilgrim, and classmate

Contents

Foreword

BRANT PITRE

Jesus of Nazareth was a man of many mysteries. He taught in puzzling parables, he performed strange signs and wonders, he asked riddle-like question after question. And his Jewish disciples and the Jewish crowds he taught—although he frequently stumped them—loved it.

But the mysteries of Jesus didn't end with his public ministry. According to the Gospels, he continued to do and say puzzling things right up to the moment of his death. One of the greatest riddles of Jesus' Passion involves the mysterious vow that he made during the Last Supper. On the night he was betrayed, toward the end of the meal, Jesus solemnly declared that he would not drink "the fruit of the vine" again until the coming of "the kingdom of God" (Luke 22:18; cf. Matthew 26:29; Mark 14:25). Later on, when he was on the way to Golgotha and the soldiers tried to offer him wine, true to his word, "he would not drink it" (Matthew 26:34; cf. Mark 14:23). On the other hand, according to the Gospel of John, at the very last moment of his life, right before he died on the cross, *Jesus requested for wine to be given to him,* saying: "I thirst" (John 19:28). Even more mysterious, after drinking the wine he declared, "It is finished," bowed his head, and gave up his spirit (John 19:30).

What are we to make of this riddle? How could Jesus vow at the Last Supper not to drink wine again, refuse it on the way to the cross, then turn around and ask for a drink right before he died? How can we reconcile Jesus' words at the Last Supper with his words on the cross? Was he breaking his vow? Or was something else going on?

To top it all off, there's one more puzzle to ponder— one that takes place *between* the upper room and Calvary. In the Garden of Gethsemane, when Jesus was praying about his death, he said something odd: "My Father, if it be possible, let *this cup* pass from me; nevertheless, not as I will, but as you will" (Matthew 26:39). And then again: "My Father, if this cannot pass *unless I drink it,* your will be done" (Matthew 26:42). Now, if you were about to be crucified, is this how you would have prayed? Why did Jesus speak about his death as "drinking" a "cup"? What cup is he talking about?

In *The Fourth Cup,* Dr. Scott Hahn gives us the keys

to unlocking this mystery—the mystery of the Last Supper and the cross. He does this in two ways: first, by going back to the Jewish roots of Jesus' words and deeds, and second, by telling you the story of his own personal journey from Protestantism to Catholicism. The result reads almost like a detective novel—an exhilarating journey of discovery that will change the way you see the Last Supper, the Passion of Christ, and the Eucharist forever.

I'll never forget the first time I heard one of Dr. Hahn's presentations on the fourth cup. I was completely blown away. It was like reading the Passion of Christ again for the first time. Don't get me wrong: it's not as if I had spent nights lying awake wondering why Jesus vowed never to drink wine again at the Last Supper and why he asked for a drink on Good Friday. Nor had I wondered all that much about why Jesus talked about his crucifixion as drinking a "cup." I just took these things for granted. But after listening to Dr. Hahn's lecture, it was like the pieces of a puzzle that I didn't even realize were there suddenly fell into place. What I *had* always wondered about was this: Why do Catholics believe that the Eucharist is *a sacrifice*? Didn't Jesus offer himself "once and for all" on Calvary? What is the link between Jesus' offering of his body and blood at the Last Supper and his death on the cross?

If you've ever wondered the same thing, or if you've

ever celebrated a Passover seder, or if you've ever just wanted to deepen your understanding of the Jewish roots of the Eucharist, then I've got one message for you, *read this book*. And don't just read it. Pray about it. Reflect on it. And share it with others.

Because if you're anything like me, once you begin to see the mystery of the Last Supper and the cross through ancient Jewish eyes, it will completely change your life. For, as Dr. Hahn shows, the Passover of Jesus that began in the upper room and was consummated on Calvary is *still with us today*. Whenever and wherever Mass is celebrated, the Paschal Mystery—that is, the "Passover" mystery—is made truly present. *The Fourth Cup* not only solves the mystery of Jesus' vow, it will also give you the missing link between the upper room and Golgotha and help you to see more clearly how the sacrifice of Christ at the Last Supper and the sacrifice of Christ on Calvary are the *same sacrifice* "poured out for the forgiveness of sins" and the redemption of the world (Matthew 26:28).

Preface

In 1989 at Marytown in Chicago I first gave a talk titled "The Fourth Cup." It was about some of the studies that had led to my conversion to Catholicism just three years before. I was, at the time, an assistant professor of religious studies at the College of St. Francis in Joliet, Illinois. I wasn't earning much. I had no tenure or publications. But I was a happy man because I was Catholic, and I wanted to tell the world. Now I had an opportunity.

It pleased me that I could tell my story to a small assembly of interested folks. It pleased me more that they responded so fervidly to my talk. Word spread, and other groups invited me to tell the tale of my "Hunt for the Fourth Cup," which I cast as a detective story, starring myself as the hapless investigator, which I am. (Peter Falk's Columbo was my model.)

That was, of course, millions of words ago, dozens

of books ago, thousands of lectures ago. I have long since lost count of the number of times I spoke on "The Fourth Cup." It's definitely in the high hundreds. I've delivered this talk on several continents—almost on site at the upper room in Jerusalem—and I've even told the tale at sea!

Last year I was talking with an old friend who's heard me give the talk on several occasions over the years. He pointed out that I never give "The Fourth Cup" the same way twice. I always cover the same time period, but I draw from different events and different ancient sources.

I acknowledged that he was right. I underwent that great adventure from 1982 to 1986, when I was a young husband, a new father, a recently ordained pastor, and a neophyte scholar. I was encountering so much of life for the first time—and then God introduced tumult and turmoil that threatened everything I was just beginning to love. I stood to lose everything that had given me comfort and confidence. My pastorate, my academic position, my friendships, even my marriage seemed capable of collapse.

How could I distill all those experiences into a single talk?

I couldn't, of course. So each time I would just tell my story, using the Passover as my theme—and I'd keep a close eye on my watch. I filled the time with whatever stories and sources surfaced in my memory.

My friend suggested that I gather those stories and sources into a single book that conveys the full sense of adventure and sleuthing.

And so I have. And here it is.

I've tried to avoid repeating tales I've already told in other books, such as *Rome Sweet Home* (coauthored with my wife, Kimberly) and *The Lamb's Supper*. The stories here are meant to supplement my earlier accounts.

When I was studying in a Protestant seminary, some of us liked to sing old-time hymns. One of them went like this:

> *I love to tell the story,*
> *'twill be my theme in glory,*
> *To tell the old, old story*
> *of Jesus and his love.*

I sang it true, all those years ago, and it's still true. After thirty years, I'm still unspeakably happy to be Catholic, but I still want to tell the world.

A NOTE ON SOURCES: The events you'll read about in this book took place a long time ago. I have, to the best of my ability, supplemented my recollections by drawing from books I was actually reading at the time. Sometimes, when memory failed, I had to draw from more recent sources, which are more familiar to me.

CHAPTER 1

What Is Finished?

I was living the dream—my dream, anyway. I had finished my bachelor's degree at the school of my choice, married the ideal woman, and I was now pursuing studies for ministry in the Presbyterian Church.

Once again, I was at the school I had carefully chosen: Gordon-Conwell Theological Seminary. My wife, Kimberly, and I had grand expectations, and the school lived up to them. We were living in a community where ordinary conversation centered on Scripture. I had classmates who shared my interests and my fervor. On the faculty were scholars of the first rank, and many were outstanding preachers as well.

My Christianity was evangelical in style, Calvinist in substance. I was aware of the religious marketplace in the Protestant world, and I chose my denomination as carefully as I chose my college and seminary. At

Gordon-Conwell—unlike most other places on earth—
I found myself among people I could call like-minded.
Together we started a weekly breakfast group and called
it the Geneva Academy, after the school founded by our
Reformation hero, John Calvin, back in the sixteenth
century.

I was on a roll with the choices I'd made. I could not
have designed an environment better suited to the development of the intellectual life I wanted. Don't get me
wrong: there were students and faculty who disagreed
with my friends and me, but we genuinely welcomed
their best arguments. "Iron sharpens iron" (Proverbs
27:17).

So the next decision that faced me was where to go
to church. Well-chosen Sunday worship would round
out the experience. At the time I thought of worship
as a mostly intellectual exercise, a concentrated Bible
study ornamented with hymns and prayers. Any hint of
ritual—liturgy—I dismissed as vain repetition, a dead
work, and precisely the sort of abomination from which
the Reformers had freed Christianity. Liturgy was for
the lost: Catholics and Orthodox and their Episcopalian
fellow travelers.

I looked around for a while before I found the ideal
church. It was in a little town about a half hour's ride
from where we were living. The pastor was my Hebrew
professor. Harvard educated and on his way to an Ox-

ford doctorate, he would become a hero to me, a friend, a model, and a mentor. He later went on to well-deserved fame—but all his great gifts were evident to me the first time I heard him preach.

The man made Scripture come alive. His erudition was vast. His mastery of the ancient languages was complete. He held degrees in physics, engineering, and divinity. It was evident. Yet he wore it lightly and delivered it with memorable humor. He labored at his sermons and always strove to find the offbeat detail—something that would arrive as a novelty and seize the congregation's attention. Then, once he had us, he kept us spellbound.

FINISH LINE

I vividly remember a sermon he preached on the Sunday preceding Easter Sunday. People who went to liturgical churches were waving fronds and calling it "Palm Sunday." We were having none of that. But even in an evangelical church we could not ignore the nearness of Easter, and the time between, so our pastor preached that palmless Sunday about the events of Good Friday.

He was always good, but he was never so good as at that hour, when he seized our attention and fixed it on the cross by which we had been saved. He was working with the richest material, more precious than gold or silver, and he didn't waste the opportunity.

He was a master preacher who calibrated his delivery with precision. But he was also open to the Holy Spirit, and so he would also speak as he was led—even if he might break his spell by doing so.

He was narrating the Passion for us, synthesizing material from all four Gospels; and as he went along he provided theological commentary between the lines of the sacred text. At every point, his explication arose as part of the drama, part of the narrative—never extraneous, always moving it forward.

Then he arrived at John 19:30, where Jesus said, "It is finished." And all of a sudden he just stopped. I thought it was for dramatic effect. And I'd wager that everyone else thought so, too.

When he resumed, however, he digressed from the homily he had been delivering. He asked us if we had ever wondered what Jesus meant by "it." *What* indeed was finished?

Okay, I had been studying homiletics. I saw what he was doing. He was asking a question of the congregation in order to set us up for the answer he would now deliver with a wallop. I was all ready. This was going to be good.

But the wallop didn't arrive. He admitted that he didn't have an answer. It was clear that this digression had not been part of his scripted sermon. It was a thought that had momentarily seized his attention.

I sat there squirming, thinking: *Of course we know what it is! It is our redemption. It is finished. Our redemption is finished.*

As if he could read my mind, however, he continued: "If you're sitting there thinking that what Jesus meant is our redemption, you'd better think again." He pointed out that, in Romans 4:25, Paul said that Jesus was *raised* for our justification. Thus, the job was "finished" not on Calvary that Friday but at the garden tomb the following Sunday.

The pastor admitted that he didn't know the answer.

He just moved on.

But I didn't. I couldn't. I don't think I heard another word of his sermon.

I was sitting there, turning the pages of my Bible and wondering: *Okay, then, what is* it? *What's finished?*

Did I sing our closing hymn? I have no idea.

Kimberly and I exited the church to a bright spring day. The pastor was standing outside, shaking hands as congregants went by.

I took his hand and said, "Don't do that!"

He was taken aback. So I explained what I meant.

He said he hadn't prepared or intended to ask that rhetorical question. He repeated his assurance that he couldn't answer it—but then he assured me that I would.

"Dive into it, Scott. Research it, and come back with an answer!"

I spent the rest of Sunday afternoon and evening diving into the text and its context. I wasn't finished by that night. I went on to study it for days, for weeks, several months, in fact. You might say that I'm still researching it today.

SEARCH AND RESEARCH

My first round of research was to return to the text and fixate on it—to read the verse in its original Greek and then in different translations, to check the classic commentaries and then the more recent interpretations. I examined the text in context. I considered the small details of the larger passage: the sponge filled with sour wine, the careful notation of the calendar date, the decision not to break the dead man's legs, and the repeated mention of the fulfillment of "Scripture."

All the footnotes and all the commentators kept directing me back to a single common theme, a story behind—or within, but certainly inseparable from—the story John was telling in his Gospel. The common theme was the Jewish festival of Passover. All the surrounding details were related to the traditional observance of the feast. I had a hunch that the key to the meaning of "It is finished" was also to be found in Passover. Jesus' death occurred during Passover, and all the eyewitnesses were eager to find significance in the providential timing of the event. The day was in the details—seemingly all the details.

The scholarly literature on Passover could fill libraries, but I entered it with abandon. The commentators, one and all, noted that Passover was the yearly feast when the people of Israel renewed their *covenant* with God. And there the commentaries rang the bell for me. Covenant was a central theme in the theology of my hero, the Reformer John Calvin—and so, indeed, in the theology of my mentor and pastor. Calvin believed that covenant was the interpretive key to the whole Bible. Covenant described the legal bond that had formed and governed humanity's relationship with God since the dawn of creation.

Whatever "it" might be that was finished, "it" was bound up in the renewal of the Old Covenant with Israel—and the sealing of the New Covenant with the Church. "It" was, moreover, something central, not peripheral, to salvation. "It" was not something I could set aside.

In time, "it" would test my connection with the life and the dream I had formed with such deliberation.

But all that came much later. The quest that began in church that Sunday was simply for a pronoun's referent. The answer, I was convinced, would be found in the Passover, the feast that became the subject of my research—and then the subject of this book.

CHAPTER 2

Passover and Covenant

Passover was the kind of topic that threatened to overwhelm a student like me. I was, of course, not the first person to recognize its supreme importance. Nor was I the first to fall into the deep well of research on the subject. Nor am I the first to feel the urgent need to set my thoughts about Passover down in a book. The volumes I found in Gordon-Conwell's library were many and well worn. I lugged them home. I read them hunched over my desk late into my nights. Then they were waiting for me when I rose from sleep early in the morning. In one of those books—or in all of them—I was convinced I would find the answer to the question of *what* was finished with Jesus' cry on the cross.

More than a century ago, the Jewish scholar Hayyim Schauss observed that Passover was, for first-century Jews as for Jews today, "more than *a* holiday; it has been *the* holiday, the festival of redemption."[1] Indeed, in the ancient Jewish sources and the modern, the language of redemption and salvation was everywhere.

To me as a Christian, that seemed providentially appropriate. If Passover is *the* festival of redemption for Jews, then Jesus, who was a Jew among Jews, would find it a fitting time to complete his redeeming work.

Jesus did not regard all elements of his heritage as equally important. He easily dispensed with some customs, while he ardently observed others. He was willing to heal on the Sabbath, for example, though the Pharisees forbade labor on that day. He was willing also to keep company with foreigners—and even foreign women—which was also forbidden by the Pharisees. Yet the Gospels show that he was regular in his Passover observance, during his childhood and during his public ministry. What, I wanted to know, did Passover mean to him, and to his neighbors, and to the eyewitnesses who testified in the Gospels?

PLAGUE GROUND

What we now call Passover the ancients called *Pesach*, and that Hebrew root means "a passing over" or "skipping" or "sparing." The feast commemorates the most dramatic of the many miracles God wrought as he liberated the Hebrews from slavery in Egypt. The Egyptian ruler, the Pharaoh, refused repeatedly to let his slaves practice their religion. God met his refusal with a series of plagues visited upon the Egyptian people; but Pharaoh remained obstinate. Chapter 12 of the Book of Exodus tells the story of the final plague, which claimed the life of every firstborn male, human and animal, in the land of Egypt.

But God gave Moses and Aaron detailed instructions about a sacrifice the Hebrews should make—the offering of a lamb, whose blood should be painted on the doorposts and lintels of their homes. As the angel of death went from one residence to the next, he "passed over" the families of the Hebrews. Their firstborn sons were spared. They were saved. They were redeemed. Their lives were bought with the blood of the Passover lamb.

It was not the end of the drama, of course. Everyone knows the rest of the story—if not from the Bible, then from Hollywood's renderings. Pharaoh let the Israelites leave his land, but then regretted his decision and pursued them. The Red Sea parted for the Israelites to pass through, and then the waters closed upon Pharaoh's army. Afterward, the Chosen People wandered for forty years, fed miraculously by God. They received the Law from him. Finally, they entered the Promised Land.

The events were unforgettable. Even so, the Chosen People were prone to forgetfulness, so God made sure that they would have a fixed means of remembrance. According to the Book of Exodus, the Lord established Passover as a festival even before the events were consummated. He said to Moses and Aaron: "This month shall be for you the beginning of months; it shall be the first month of the year for you" (Exodus 12:2).

Moses then relayed the Lord God's detailed instructions for a ritual meal, to be celebrated every year on the anniversary of Israel's deliverance from Egypt. The main course would always be the lamb whose blood was smeared by the door. God specified the age and condition of the lamb. He prescribed the method of preparation and cooking. He indicated also what the side dishes should be: bitter herbs and unleavened bread.

Every ingredient in the meal was a mnemonic device. The herbs were to remind the people of the bitterness of their life in slavery. The unleavened bread recalled the hurried preparation of that last meal in Egypt; there was no time to wait for the dough to rise. The lamb? Well, he died in place of the firstborn.

The commandment was clear. This feast was to be observed in perpetuity. "This day shall be for you a memorial day, and you shall keep it as a feast to the LORD; throughout your generations you shall observe it as an ordinance for ever" (Exodus 12:14). Every year, every household in Israel was to do this in remembrance of the Lord and his mighty deeds.

There is, in the Book of Exodus and in the later literature of the rabbis, a great emphasis on the exactness of the ritual. There was even a scripted catechetical exchange of questions and answers.

> And when you come to the land which the LORD will give you, as he has promised, you shall keep this service. And when your children say to you, "What do you mean by this service?" you shall say, "It is the sacrifice of the LORD's passover, for he passed over the houses of the people of Israel in Egypt, when he slew the Egyptians but spared our houses." (Exodus 12:25–27)

Nothing could be so clear as the prescription for this feast. It should have been fail-safe. The people of Israel could never forget the marvels the Lord had done for them in the Exodus. Could they?

B'RITH OF FRESH AIR

The Lord God, for his part, made clear that he heard their complaints and rescued them because of "his covenant with" their ancestors, "with Abraham, with Isaac, and with Jacob" (Exodus 2:24; see also 6:5). More than a dozen times, the Book of Exodus reminds readers that "the covenant" is the reason God acts in Israel's favor.

"Covenant" is the English translation of the Hebrew word *b'rith*. Greek-speaking Jews rendered it as *diathēkē*. The word provided, for Israel, the interpretive key to their history as a people. All biblical religion is based on this notion. Christians have, from the first generation, divided the Scriptures (and indeed all history) into the Old Covenant and the New Covenant (see Galatians 4:24; 2 Corinthians 3:6, 14; Hebrews 8:6–9, 13). In the West, we sometimes miss the meaning—and the structural unity—of Scripture because of the choice to translate the Greek *diathēkē* as "testament" rather than "covenant" in the title of each portion of our Bible.

When God "remembers" his covenant, he is invoking the act by which he established a kinship bond with his Chosen People. God had, in fact, established such a bond with all humanity at the creation of Adam and Eve[2]; but they violated the covenant and separated themselves and all their descendants from God's glory. For with every covenant bond come mutual obligations. Those who fulfill the obligations enjoy the blessings of the covenant. Those who fail to fulfill the obligations break the covenant and suffer the resulting disasters. We see the classic statement of this in Deuteronomy 11, when God says:

> Behold, I set before you this day a blessing and a curse: the blessing, if you obey the command-ments of the LORD your God, which I com-mand you this day, and the curse, if you do not obey the commandments of the LORD your God. (Deuteronomy 11:26–28)

The consequence of Adam's disobedience was es-trangement from God. Yet God reached out, again and again, to reestablish the bond with humanity. He made a covenant with the family of Noah, and then again with Abraham and his offspring. Now, at the Exodus, he "remembered" his covenant with Abraham, invok-ing it as the reason for Israel's redemption.

In the Bible, nothing is more serious than a cov-enant. It is sealed by a solemn ritual act, the equivalent of an oath invoking God. The details of the ritual signify the gravity of the act. Blood is the sign of the covenant renewed at Passover. When Moses later gave Israel the Law, he called it "the book of the covenant"; and he took blood from a sacrifice and "threw it upon the people, and said, 'Behold the blood of the covenant which the LORD has made with you in accordance with all these words'" (Exodus 24:7–8).

The early Christians retained this keen sense of the centrality of the covenant in Scripture. That sense, however, has waxed and waned in biblical interpretation since then. John Calvin and other Protestant Reformers emphasized the legal and juridical dimension of God's acts, and so they launched a revival of interest in the biblical covenants. As a seminarian at Gordon-Conwell, I enjoyed the choicest fruits of that revival. My pastor was young and just emerging as a widely respected covenant theologian; his great mentor, Dr. Meredith Kline, was also on the faculty. Covenant scholarship was even enjoying a revival among Catholics. As a seminarian I was deeply anti-Catholic but nevertheless aware of the work of Dennis McCarthy, a Jesuit at the Pontifical Biblical Institute.

PASCH, PRESENCE, AND FUTURE

The notion of covenant was so obvious that it could not be ignored for long. And yet it has been—not only by Christians but in the ancient world as well. Although God remained faithful, his people fell repeatedly into sin, thus bringing upon themselves curses of a catastrophic scale: the Great Flood, slavery in Egypt, forty years of wandering in the desert, the crackup of a kingdom, and long years of exile in Babylon.

The Book of Exodus was explicit: Passover should be

observed every year as a renewal of the covenant. Moses presents the ritual as scripted by God himself. Indeed, in the later books of the Hebrew Scriptures, we see Israel observing the Passover in this way. While Moses was still alive, the people kept the festival in the Sinai desert. When Joshua entered the Promised Land, the people celebrated Passover at Gilgal (Joshua 5:10).

But centuries passed. In fact, the better part of a millennium passed, and the people felt secure in the land they had been given. It seems that, along the way, they forgot their own story. They forgot the covenant.

The Second Book of Chronicles shows us the decadence of the latter days of the kingdom. In chapter 34 we see the high priest Hilkiah "discover" the Book of the Law, which had somehow fallen into disuse. Hilkiah reads the book and learns—to his horror—that the people had been failing miserably in their obligations to God. He informs the king, Josiah, who is similarly horrified. Josiah mandates a religious revival, which begins with the celebration of Passover (2 Chronicles 35:1).

Passover was celebrated in Jerusalem. It was, in fact, one of the three pilgrim festivals of Judaism—the three times every year when every Israelite male was required by law to go to Jerusalem for religious observance (see Exodus 23:14–17).

And Passover was, by far, the greatest of those feasts.

SCOTT HAHN

The Prophet Ezekiel envisioned it ideally as a time of joy, when all the people ate to satiety, and the Messiah-King picked up the tab (Ezekiel 45:18–24). It was joyful, but in a measured way, and solemn. The feast of Shavuot (Pentecost), which was also held in Jerusalem, was known for its revelry. But the party atmosphere was not proper for Passover. Its joy was intensely religious.

King Josiah's reform may have restored religious observance to Jerusalem. But it was too little, too late, and not long afterward the lands were conquered and the people exiled. Still, the reform had its lasting effects. We're told that when the people returned from exile they immediately resumed the proper celebration of Passover (Ezra 6:19–20).

The festival was established for two purposes: to make remembrance, and to give thanks. We keep national holidays for the same reasons today. But we need to make an important distinction when we examine the festivals of Israel, because their idea of *memory* is profoundly different from ours.

In biblical religion, memory is not simply the psychological act of recalling a past event. Rather, it is the re-presentation of the event. Thus, even today, when Jews observe the Passover they speak of themselves as participants in the Exodus, and they give thanks for their deliverance. When the son asks his father about the reason for their celebration, the father responds with

34

a line from the Torah: "It is because of what the LORD did for me when I came out of Egypt" (Exodus 13:8). Liberation belonged not only to the last generation that lived enslaved in Egypt. The event of Passover belonged to all Jews collectively and each Jew individually.

It must have marked one of the vivid memories in the life of ordinary Jews living in or around Jerusalem during the time of Jesus. For those who lived in the hinterlands, it began with a difficult journey. Once they arrived in the city, the festival occupied eight full days. "Passover" properly refers to the first day, when the lambs were sacrificed and eaten. For seven days afterward, however, the celebration continued with the Feast of Unleavened Bread. The two festivals were closely related, and Jews used the names interchangeably to describe the extended observance.

Jerusalem's population swelled, with people living uncomfortably in close quarters. Everyone had to find a place to eat the Passover meal—and a group of no fewer than ten people with whom to share a lamb. The first-century historian Josephus notes one year when there were 255,660 lambs slaughtered and more than two million people present. Even if Josephus was grossly exaggerating—even if we reduce his estimates by half—we're still talking about an enormous crowd. For at least a week every year, Jerusalem became one of the most populous cities in the ancient world.

The Temple regions bustled with nonstop activity. All twenty-four divisions of Levites (the priestly tribe) were expected to report for work. Some sang, others slaughtered the lambs, and some caught the blood in trays made of silver or gold. Priests then threw the lambs' blood and fat onto the altar.

But the sacrifice was complete only with the eating of the lamb. That was the act that renewed the covenant. That was the act that constituted Israel as a nation. That was the act by which individual Jews knew communion with one another and with God. Thus, the rabbinic sources directed that no Jew should be excluded because of poverty. Everyone should be able to share in the Passover lamb—a portion at least the size of an olive—and in the four cups of wine that punctuated the Passover menu.

Those days would have been vivid memories from Jesus' childhood, and from the early lives of the Apostles. The city was suffused with excitement, exuberant confidence, and national pride, and the celebration lasted for days. We should not be surprised that acts of rebellion against the occupying powers sometimes took place during Passover.[3] The ancient sources preserve the common belief among Jews that God's anointed, the Messiah, would manifest himself during Passover.

Nonetheless, even the Romans recognized the supreme importance of the Passover and paid their respect in token ways. They might, for example, release a prisoner to honor the day.

A PASSION FOR PASSOVER

In that first week of research, night and day, I learned what I could from the historic traces of the ancient celebration of Passover. The remains were sometimes elusive and elliptical, but also strongly suggestive of a story I thought I knew well—a story that ended when its protagonist said, "It is finished."

In the ancient Passover there was blood; there was the covenant; there was the lamb of God; there was salvation, redemption, liberation; there were prisoners set free. Each detail illuminated some aspect of the Passion of Jesus.

It was all, moreover, in keeping with what I'd long known about the covenant. There was a familiar quality to everything I read, and yet it also seemed to arrive as something utterly new.

Certainly, "it" was finished long ago. But I felt that my understanding of it was just beginning.

CHAPTER 3

A Typical Sacrifice

Conversation at Gordon-Conwell, as I said, often gravitated toward the interpretation of Scripture. Certain issues were always controversial, and these included even some basic principles. Both students and faculty differed among themselves, for example, about how to read the Old Testament. The matter of typology was especially vexatious.

Typology is the study of persons, events, or things in the Old Testament as foreshadowings—prototypes—that are fulfilled in the New Testament. All Christians agree that Jesus is prefigured in the Hebrew Scriptures. Jesus himself revealed this. He referred to Jonah (Matthew 12:39), Solomon (Matthew 12:42), the Temple (John 2:19), and the brazen serpent (John 3:14) as "signs" that pointed forward to him. The first Christians, too, read the Scriptures in this way. Philip saw Jesus prefigured in the Suffering Servant described by the Prophet

Isaiah (Acts 8:32–35). Paul taught that "Adam . . . was a type of the one who was to come" (Romans 5:14). The First Letter of Peter presents Noah's flood as a type of baptism (1 Peter 3:20–21).

The fact of biblical types is not controversial. Among my friends at Gordon-Conwell, the controversy swirled around the degree to which a reader should be free to identify types in the Old Testament. I taunted some classmates for being typological maximalists (or "hyper-typers"), looking for Jesus—and finding him—in almost every passage and precept of Israel's law and history. I had other friends, however, who held that we should identify as types *only* those Old Testament figures that the New Testament itself identifies as types.

Passover itself was safe because it fell into this latter category. No less an authority than Saint Paul put it there, in his First Letter to the Corinthians. It could not be stated more plainly: "Christ, our Passover, has been sacrificed" (1 Corinthians 5:7). The central term, *pascha* in Greek, has been variously translated as "Passover" or "Paschal lamb." Either translation is valid, because Jews at the time used the word *pascha* to denote both the feast and its characteristic sacrifice, the lamb. The terms in the following sentence make clear that Paul is speaking, broadly, of the "festival" that had been traditionally observed with "unleavened bread."

Paul distinguishes between the Christian fulfillment

("*our* Passover") and its ancient Jewish type. He places the two in explicit contrast, using the words "old" and "new." Yet he recognizes also the continuity from promise to fulfillment. Certain terms and images remain constant: "Passover," "sacrifice," "unleavened bread."

Through my study of the Passover, I was beginning to see that typology was operative to a much greater extent than I had been willing to admit. The ancient Passover prefigured salvation in Christ not simply by providing a name but rather by providing the richest possible context for our understanding. I began to see how carefully God, in his providence, had prepared the way for his Son. Earlier in the same Letter to the Corinthians, Paul had signaled as much, saying: "But we impart a secret and hidden wisdom of God, which God decreed before the ages for our glorification" (1 Corinthians 2:7). The typology of the Old Testament, made clear in the New Testament, shows the dynamic unity of God's plan from creation through redemption. What God had decreed from the beginning played out gradually in fulfillment. The signs were indeed everywhere in the Old Testament.

ECLIPSE OF SACRIFICE

My study of the Passover caused me to make a closer examination of terms I had long taken for granted. In presenting the Passover as a type, Paul spoke most directly of sacrifice; and I knew, of course, that sacrifice was at the heart of Old Testament worship. I knew, moreover, that the New Testament portrayed Israel's sacrificial system itself as a type. The idea is most explicit in the Letter to the Hebrews, which examines Christ's death as a sacrificial offering. Like the Old Testament rites, Jesus' death involved the shedding of blood and the offering of a body. Like the Old Testament rites, his death sealed a covenant between heaven and earth, between God and his people.

Unlike the Old Testament rites, however, Jesus' sacrifice was all-sufficient and unrepeatable. "He has no need, like those high priests, to offer sacrifices daily, first for his own sins and then for those of the people; he did this once for all when he offered up himself" (Hebrews 7:27; see also 9:12, 9:26, and 10:10).

I was beginning to realize how revolutionary Christianity must have seemed in the ancient world. Scholars often point out Jesus' influence on subsequent intellectual history. But that's something we see only now, in retrospect. In the first and second centuries, the most striking thing about Christianity was probably how little it looked like a *religion*.

All the major religions of the first century, and all the popular cults, practiced blood sacrifice—the ritual slaughter of animals for religious purposes. Romans did. Greeks did. Jews did. Nor is this a phenomenon peculiar to Western peoples. In the same century, but living in total isolation from the Greco-Roman world, the Mayans offered animal (and human) sacrifices on altars in Mesoamerica. Sacrifice of this kind was so ubiquitous as to seem essential to religion, a defining characteristic.

The New Testament authors assume that their readers think of religion in terms of blood sacrifice. Yet they also present Christianity as a religion whose only sacrifice was "once for all" and had already been completed.

For Christians, Jesus' death had put an end to the sacrifices offered in the Jerusalem Temple. Indeed, less than forty years after Jesus' death, the Temple itself was utterly destroyed, never to be rebuilt. The Greek and Roman religions, meanwhile, have all passed away. Religions founded since the first century (i.e., rabbinic Judaism and Islam) are uniformly nonsacrificial. Today, there's hardly a place on earth where animal sacrifice is practiced.

This puts us, I believe, at a disadvantage as we try to understand Paul's discussion of sacrifice. Today we think of worship as an unbloody event. We read Paul's passages about altars, priests, and offerings, and we translate them instantly to metaphor. We don't see Jerusalem's streams flowing red with blood as the priests went about their business of bleeding hundreds of thousands of lambs every year at Passover.

As I studied the Passover anew, I wanted to recover the sense that Paul had when he first realized that "Christ, our Passover, has been sacrificed." I wanted to know what sacrifice meant for him and his contemporaries. I wanted to know what sacrifice meant in the context of Passover, the feast of redemption.

SEALED WITH A CURSE

Sacrifice represents the greatest disconnect between us and our remote ancestors in biblical religion. Yet it's there in the background or foreground of almost every book of our Bible. It is the act that seals and renews every covenant between God and his people. God and his mediators took exacting care in specifying the small details—who, what, when, and where—of every offering.

The "why," however, is most puzzling for us. The ancients took the reasons for granted, as too obvious to mention. So we often have to read between the lines. To us moderns, animal sacrifice can seem like an empty ritual, the satisfaction of a primitive impulse—violent, wasteful, and brutal. But for Israel it was anything but empty. It was overflowing with meaning.

Sacrifice was the principal way of ratifying, renewing, and repairing the relational bond between God and his people. Our word "sacrifice" comes from a Latin compound meaning "to make holy" or "to set apart." (The Hebrew equivalent is *corban,* and it has the same connotations.) By offering a sacrifice, a man was swearing an oath-in-action, and invoking God as his witness.

Consider the covenant made between God and Abram (who was later to become Abraham). God commands Abram to gather a variety of animals for sacrifice: "a heifer three years old, a she-goat three years old, a ram three years old, a turtledove, and a young pigeon" (Genesis 15:9). Abram cuts the larger animals in half and divides their pieces, then stands watch over them. In time, God sent fire between the halves of the animals, and he announced the terms of the covenant, both the blessings and the curses.

In a most basic sense, such a sacrifice returns to God what is rightly his. The one who sacrifices recognizes that God is the creator and sovereign ruler of the universe. All life belongs to him. A sacrifice, then, is a form of worship, praise, and thanksgiving.

But there is much more going on—much more signified by the sacrificial victims. There is an implied threat coded into the violence of sacrifice. Every covenant bore both blessings and curses—blessings upon fulfillment and curses upon nonfulfillment. The blood of the animals represented the new family bond that was established through the covenant. The partners were now "blood kin." That's the blessing, the upside. But the slaughtered animals also represented the consequences of any infidelity to the terms of the covenant. To violate the covenant was to desecrate an oath sworn before God. Infidelity was something akin to blasphemy, and so it merited death. No one who had offered the sacrifice could claim ignorance, for they had presented the terms of the covenant upon the altar.

There was nothing casual about God's covenants. They were life-and-death matters. They were always sealed by blood, which bespoke a new kinship bond. The blood also signified the power of God, who gives life and deals death. The prophets proclaimed as much in their oracles: "because of the blood of my covenant with you, I will set your captives free from the waterless pit" (Zechariah 9:11). The blood of the covenant testified to God's power to deliver his people.

Each victim stood as a warning, but also as a proxy. Whenever God's people violated their covenants— whenever they fell into sin—they offered sacrifice in order to repair and restore their bond with God. Recognizing that their sins deserved death, they offered an animal as their substitute. Their sacrifice was a vivid expression of their sorrow.

The Passover lamb was clearly a substitutionary sacrifice. God had demanded the lives of every firstborn male in the land of Egypt. The lamb's blood on the doorpost was a sign that the obligation had been satisfied. But, we should ask, why weren't the Hebrews simply exempt because of their ethnicity? Indeed they were not exempt. They had fallen under the curse because they had violated the covenant. Their ancestors, the sons of Jacob, had sinned grievously by selling their brother Joseph into slavery. The Hebrews of later generations sinned further, and still more grievously, by worshipping the animal-gods of Egypt (see Exodus 12:12, Joshua 24:14–15, Ezekiel 20:7–8).

The Hebrews were delivered from death and liberated from Egypt not because they deserved to be saved, not because they were innocent, but because God is merciful. At the Passover—and, later, by means of the sacrificial system—the Lord required them to "put to death" the idols they had once adored. He required them also to witness their own execution with the animal as their substitute. The medieval rabbi Nachmanides called such animal sacrifice an "execution in effigy." The modern Jewish scholar Joshua Berman explains that the action is at once punitive and remedial. "As he stands before God in the Temple and witnesses his own execution by proxy for sins he committed, the owner of the offering is meant to reach a new awareness of his obligations to God so that his breach will not be repeated."[1]

There is still another—and I would say higher—level of meaning in animal sacrifice. Yes, the animal stands as a warning. And, yes, the animal dies as a substitute.

But the animal also dies as a *representative* of the person who makes the offering. The animal represents a gift of one's entire life to God. When a father entered the courtyard of the Temple and laid down the Passover lamb for his family, he was laying down his life. That's why the Passover sacrifice was so dramatic, so solemn, and so cathartic for its participants. It's not just that the blood of a quarter million lambs was flowing like a river into the Kidron Valley. It's not just that fat was flying on the Temple's massive altar. The drama was in the offering represented in all that life laid down—all the sin forgiven, all the tomorrows redeemed.

I'm not saying that everyone who entered the Temple was thinking pious thoughts. In Jerusalem in the first century—as in Massachusetts in the 1980s—God's people often showed up to worship distracted and dull. They went through the motions. They followed their routines. That's what people tend to do.

Sometimes, in fact, they do this for a long time, and then they lose interest in worship altogether. The pages of the Bible are replete with reminders from God about the meaning of sacrifice, and the purpose of sacrifice, and the place of sacrifice in the grand scheme of things. "For I desire steadfast love and not sacrifice, the knowledge of God, rather than burnt offerings" (Hosea 6:6; see also Matthew 9:13, 12:7). It's not that God wanted his people to stop offering their victims at the Temple.

No, he wanted each sacrifice to serve its purpose. He wanted them to offer each sacrifice wholeheartedly and then be changed by it. The divine case is made most thoroughly in one of the Psalms of David.

"I do not reprove you for your sacrifices;
   your burnt offerings are continually before me.
I will accept no bull from your house,
   nor he-goat from your folds.
For every beast of the forest is mine,
   the cattle on a thousand hills.
I know all the birds of the air,
   and all that moves in the field is mine.
If I were hungry, I would not tell you;
   for the world and all that is in it is mine.
Do I eat the flesh of bulls,
   or drink the blood of goats?
Offer to God a sacrifice of thanksgiving,
   and pay your vows to the Most High;
   and call upon me in the day of trouble;
I will deliver you, and you shall glorify me."
But to the wicked God says:
   "What right have you to recite my statutes,
   or take my covenant on your lips?
For you hate discipline,
   and you cast my words behind you."

(Psalm 50:8–17)

The Lord God makes clear that he instituted sacrifice not for *his* own sake but for ours. He doesn't get hungry or thirsty. He didn't actually consume the victims that he was given. The action was symbolic. In the very next Psalm in the canon, King David observes that God takes "no delight in sacrifice" (Psalm 51:16). God taught Israel to sacrifice not so that his Chosen People would be humiliated but so that they would learn to lay down their lives, to turn away from sin, and to live in the covenant. "The sacrifice acceptable to God is a broken spirit; a broken and contrite heart" (Psalm 51:17).

Thus, at the first Passover, God's intention was not simply to liberate slaves from Egypt. He wanted to liberate Israel from sin—freeing his people to give their lives sacrificially. That was a distinction too easily forgotten, as we can see in the Psalms' reminders.

When "Christ, our Passover," was sacrificed, he said, "It is finished." And with that the curtain was torn in the Temple (Matthew 27:51). The Temple was de-commissioned, and the ancient types were fulfilled. With the mystery of this new Passover, the sacrificial system had reached the end of its usefulness.

CHAPTER 4

Rite Turns

I don't want to give the impression that I had bound-less leisure time during seminary. I didn't, and so I couldn't give free rein to my curiosity. The curriculum at Gordon-Conwell was demanding, and I was the kind of student who pushed hard anyway. As the semester arced downward toward finals, I burrowed into the nec-essary books—and put aside my fascination with the question posed by my professor-pastor. I returned my Passover volumes to the library, hoping to take up the matter on another day.

At the end of three years I left my clean, well-lighted place in seminary and went forward into pastoral min-istry, hired by Trinity Presbyterian Church in Fairfax, Virginia, and ordained as a Presbyterian minister. There I had a pulpit, and I had classrooms, and I began to live a life that I hoped would be much like that of the man who had been my pastor in Massachusetts, a life with pastoral and academic dimensions. I longed to continue my scholarly researches, but I also wanted to apply them to real life in real time.

Every pastor brings his particular interests to the pulpit, and I brought mine. My interest in the covenant did not end with graduation. If anything, it had intensified now that I had daily opportunities to teach others and weekly opportunities to preach.

As a pastor, moreover, I had the obligation to baptize and preside at the "Lord's Supper." While our church generally rejected the kind of elaborate liturgy observed by Catholics, Orthodox, and Anglicans, we stood by the practice of baptism and the Lord's Supper, as these were the only two sacraments recognized by John Calvin.

Baptism, as I had learned from my professors at Gordon-Conwell, was the ordinary way to enter the covenant. Jesus commanded his disciples to baptize (Matthew 28:19), and the disciples were faithful to that command (see Acts 2:41, 8:36–38, 18:8, and many other places). The ritual marked the beginning of a new life for believers—a new relationship with God. Circumcision had formerly been the way for a male to enter into covenant with God. Scripture even identifies the Old Covenant by its rite of initiation. Stephen the Deacon referred to Judaism as "the covenant of circumcision" (Acts 7:8).

In the New Covenant, however, Baptism clearly

assumes the place formerly occupied by circumcision. Saint Paul made the connection explicit:

> In [Christ] also you were circumcised with a circumcision made without hands, by putting off the body of flesh in the circumcision of Christ; and you were buried with him in baptism, in which you were also raised with him through faith in the working of God, who raised him from the dead. (Colossians 2:11–12)

Baptism, then, is the "circumcision of Christ," now undergone by followers of Christ. It is the seal of the New Covenant, as circumcision was the seal of the Old. This is what I preached from my pulpit, telling as much of the biblical story as I thought my congregation could stand . . . and then adding just a little more.

So, if Baptism was the seal of the covenant, what then was the Lord's Supper? How should we understand our reenactment of Jesus' last meal before his Passion? And how should I preach about it? The matter was of more-than-academic interest to me now. It was no longer driven just by my curiosity and my library card but rather by my care for the souls of others. I was leading my congregation to a deeper understanding of the covenant because I considered it essential to the experience and conduct of a deeply Christian life.

All of my seminary research came back to me as I prepared to give my first sermon on the Lord's Supper. Some Protestant churches offered weekly communion. Ours, at the time, did not. But I wanted the congregation to know what this biblical rite meant in its original biblical context.

So I began to set down my notes. If Baptism was the seal of the covenant, then the Lord's Supper was the means of covenant renewal. It was the way that each Christian individually, and all of us collectively, reaffirmed and strengthened our belonging to God's family, his people.

The establishment of this rite loomed large for me because it was the one and only time that the Gospels record Jesus using the word "covenant."

> And he took a cup, and when he had given thanks he gave it to them, and they all drank of it. And he said to them, "This is my blood of the covenant, which is poured out for many." (Mark 14:23–24)

The word appears elsewhere in the New Testament; but in the Gospels—and from the mouth of Jesus—we have only this one instance. If the covenant was as central to biblical religion as I said it was, then this was a pivotal verse.

In defining the contents of the cup, Jesus is clearly echoing the words spoken by Moses in the Sinai desert, when he sprinkled blood upon the people: "Behold the blood of the covenant" (Exodus 24:8).

Luke's Gospel records a further elaboration of Jesus' words of blessing. After declaring the cup of wine to be "the new covenant in my blood" (Luke 22:20), Jesus adds, "Do this, as often as you drink it, in remembrance of me" (1 Corinthians 11:25). Again, this echoes words spoken at the Exodus in regard to the Passover: "This day shall be for you a memorial" (Exodus 12:14). Jesus is establishing a new rite of remembrance and renewal, and he is doing it in the context of Israel's ancient rite. The scene is a Passover meal.

What was going on here? And how should I present it in a sermon? I used covenantal terms. At the first Passover, God established a family bond by means of a blood covenant. The ritual and the meal were symbolic of the flesh-and-blood communion shared between Israel and God.

At the Lord's Supper, Jesus was establishing a stronger bond—unbreakable, in fact. He is the eternal Son of God, and he now stood in our stead as the Son of Man. He was infinitely greater than Moses, and so his covenant was of an entirely new and greater order. Moses brought about communion in Israel—and communion with God—when the people gathered in Jerusalem to eat the Passover lamb. Now Jesus brought about communion in his Church when the people gathered to eat his "flesh" and drink his "blood" at the meal he declared to be his New Covenant.

I put the words "flesh" and "blood" here in quotes because the action was, for us as Presbyterians, purely symbolic. The meal was valuable as a sign, and it was perhaps the most important sign in the world, but it was only a sign.

SEDER RITE WORDS

As I prepared the sermon, I found myself resuming the research I had set aside in seminary. Again I took up the study of the traditional Passover meal, so that I could discover more about the original context of Jesus' action.

The ritual meal for Passover is called the *seder,* and the document that prescribes its order is known as the *haggadah.* The basic structure of the seder appears to have been formalized long before the time of Jesus. In fact, the Gospel accounts assume that readers are already familiar with the structure of the seder.

Today we know about that structure mostly from the Mishnah, the earliest compilation of Jewish traditions, set down by the rabbis around A.D. 200. The Mishnah corroborates the accounts in the Gospels—and fills in many of the details the evangelists took for granted.

The seder was divided into four parts or courses.

First, the preliminary course consisted of a festival blessing (*kiddush*) spoken over the first cup of wine, followed by the serving of a dish of herbs.

The second course included a recital of the Passover narrative along with the Psalm known as the "Little Hallel" (Psalm 113; *hallel* means "praise"). Then came the drinking of the second cup of wine.

The third course was the main meal, consisting of lamb and unleavened bread, after which was drunk the third cup of wine, known as the "cup of blessing."

The Passover climaxed with the singing of the "Great Hallel" (Psalms 114–118) and the drinking of the fourth cup of wine.

The Mishnah attributes its seder instructions to no less a teacher than Gamaliel the Great, a contemporary of Jesus, recognized in the New Testament as the teacher of Saint Paul (see Acts 22:3) and indeed the greatest teacher of his time (see Acts 5:34). Gamaliel pays close attention to the ritual signs—the foods and the cups— and he insists that they must be interpreted aloud.

> Rabban Gamaliel said, Whoever did not say these three things on Passover did not fulfill

his obligation: sacrifice, unleavened bread, and bitter herbs.[1]

Thus we see that the seder was not celebrated in silence. The leader of the meal—usually the family patriarch, or the community's rabbi—customarily interpreted the items on the table. He needed not just to lift the cups and the unleavened bread and put them on display but also to "say" those three things. He needed to explain their relevance. The people in attendance had to understand how each item commemorated the conditions of the original Passover.

That brief, often-cited passage from the Mishnah was giving me new insight into the Gospels' narrative of the Last Supper. Jesus' words and actions seem mysterious and elliptical. Some details would be familiar from all the Passovers that had gone before: the cups, the Psalms, the blessings. But others must have seemed strange and even shocking: pronouncing bread to be his body, for example, and wine to be his blood.

Yet, even so, it all made a kind of sense. The man who led the meal was expected—he was required—to "say" something about the elements on the table before him. He needed to explain their relevance in light of the new Passover.

I was not the first to notice that the Gospel accounts

of the Last Supper seem to provide a haggadah, a narrative of origins, for the Christian Passover, a haggadah for the New Covenant.

FROM WEAK TO WEEK

I tried my best to communicate all of these discoveries to the people in my congregation. My research overflowed that one sermon on the Lord's Supper—and, in fact, filled many others afterward. For me this was confirmation of my belief in the importance of the covenant. When people in the pews began to see what God had been doing, and how he'd been doing it, they wanted to know more. They came to me with questions. Their questions drove me to further research.

Our church's infrequent communion—we offered it only four times a year—seemed woefully inadequate to me. If our Sunday worship was our means of renewing and strengthening our covenant bond, shouldn't we be communing more often? I proposed that we change. In fact, I proposed that we move from quarterly communion to weekly communion—a proposal that intrigued some people and made others *very* uneasy.

I began also to supplement our order of service with many passages from Scripture. If the Gospel narrative was a haggadah, as I believed it was, then we should be using it for guidance every time we commemorated our new Passover. We should be telling the story of Jesus' last seder and imitating his actions. So our Sunday service took up new forms, a new solemnity, and a new life.

It did not occur to me at the time that I was, day by day, approximating the practice of the Catholic Church. If you had suggested that, I would have been appalled. I was still firmly anti-Catholic in my theology—and passionately so in my prejudice. In any event, I had never attended a Mass, so I wasn't getting my ideas from Rome. I was getting them from the Bible. If the Catholics were right about this, then it was not so much to their credit as to our shame.

Some members of my congregation, however, were ex-Catholics, and they were not buying it. They warned me about my "Romish" tendencies. What I was proposing, they said, was beginning to look like what they had left.

I took their concerns seriously, and I always followed up. Every objection pressed me on to more reading. I would start with the Scriptures, and then consult the classic commentaries. But I also began to explore the works of the rabbis, and the relevant works of archaeology—and these led me to extensive reading of the ancient Christian writers, the so-called Fathers of the first, second, third, and fourth centuries.

I found nothing in these sources to slow me down as

I changed our Sunday worship. The more I learned, in fact, the more I wanted to share with the people whom God had entrusted to my care. This is what I had been called to the ministry for. This is what I had been ordained for. This was my definition of joy. From the faces of most of the folks in the congregation—and from the majority of conversations I had on the steps of the church—I knew I was not enjoying it all by myself.

People were finding new meaning and life in the covenant and in our increasingly covenantal worship.

PASCH FAIL?

The most serious objection I faced is one that I should bring up here, since it affects the very premise of my investigations.

There was, through the twentieth century, a trend among critical scholars to insist that the Last Supper was *not* a Passover meal. It was, according to this theory, a solemn banquet celebrated close to the day of the feast, but it was *not* a Passover meal.

If the critics were right, then surely I was wrong about the context, the covenantal content, and the deepest meaning of the Passover. If they were right, I had no business increasing the Paschal character of our Presbyterian Sunday service.

I knew that the work of scholars was hardly infallible. I knew also that academic trends did not guarantee veracity or even consensus. Even so, I took the matter seriously. If they were right and I was wrong, I wanted to know it. I had no desire to lead my congregation astray. And I had every motivation to stay on the right path myself.

CHAPTER 5

The Paschal Shape
of the Gospels

In the twenty-first century, we like to think of ourselves as shrewd consumers of news—and even history. We're skeptical of traditions. We like to think we set a high bar of veracity for evidence. But we have traditions of our own, and among them is the annual proliferation of articles and television specials that claim to disprove the New Testament claims about Jesus. They begin to appear midway through Lent, and they grow numerous during Holy Week. It's a kind of secular liturgy, with its own proclamations, its own appeals to authority, and its own formative purpose. Among the usual targets is the Passover character of the Last Supper.

One such headline, just a few years ago, asked, "The Last Supper—A Passover Seder?"[1] A procession of skeptical experts was summoned to testify before the author came to a predictably negative conclusion.

This is not news, and it's not new. It was a pattern

already established, in academia and in media, in those long-ago years when I was a pastor. In 1984 a Jewish scholar named Baruch Bokser summarized the recent research and concluded: "The current state of scholarship tends to argue against the identification of the Last Supper as a seder."[2]

The New Testament authors, however, did not seem to harbor any doubt. The Gospel According to Mark—which is often tagged by skeptics as the earliest and most reliable of the Gospels—is unambiguous in its testimony. The evangelist states plainly that the Last Supper takes place "on the first day of Unleavened Bread, when they sacrificed the Passover lamb" (Mark 14:12). The disciples say they are going to "prepare . . . to eat the Passover" (ibid.). Jesus himself describes the action in the same terms: "I am to eat the Passover with my disciples" (Mark 14:14). And, if that were not clear enough, the evangelist goes on to tell us, "the disciples set out and went to the city . . . and they prepared the Passover" (Mark 14:16). In five verses, Mark date-stamps the event four times.

The first three Gospels, in fact, present the Last Supper in strikingly similar ways. They tend to track closely in their presentation of all the events in Jesus' ministry. This is why scholars refer to Matthew, Mark, and Luke as the "Synoptic Gospels"—from a Greek word that means "seeing together." When they differ, it is usually because one evangelist is including details that the others omitted. Thus, for example, only Luke mentions that Jesus told his disciples: "I have earnestly desired to eat this Passover with you before I suffer" (Luke 22:15). Only Matthew tells us that, in the days before the Last Supper, Jesus made this rather specific prediction: "after two days the Passover is coming, and the Son of man will be delivered up to be crucified" (Matthew 26:2).

They differ in the specifics they choose to bring to the foreground, but all three of the Synoptics agree that the Last Supper was a Passover meal.

So what's the problem?

Well, the critics identify several problems.

The first is that the narratives fail to mention several of the menu items necessary for the seder. We search in vain for any word of bitter herbs or the sacrificial lamb. If those items were absent—and if Jesus did not speak of them—then the Last Supper failed two of Rabban Gamaliel's three requirements for a valid Passover.

Critics also note that the disciples never pose the scripted questions to their Master, and the Master never tells the story of the Exodus. These details are indeed absent from the narratives, but that hardly means they were missing from the event. The Gospels, in fact, *never* give us exhaustive reportage. Luke, for example, offers very few particulars in the story of Mary's purification and Jesus' presentation (see Luke 2:22–24). In a similar way, he provides little in the way of liturgical context when he tells of Jesus' teaching in the synagogue (Luke 4:16–27).

The Gospel narratives, especially in the Synoptics, are spare, light on detail. The evangelists assume that their readers have at least a glancing familiarity with Jewish customs. Thus, they assume that the Passover and the seder—like the synagogue liturgy and the ritual of purification—need not be explained.

The omissions hardly make a case for rejecting the Synoptic Gospels' placement of the Last Supper on the night of Passover. The omissions, however, are not the critics' most critical issue.

GO FOURTH

There are, of course, more than three Gospels. There is a fourth Gospel, and it is rarely "synoptic" with the others. The Gospel According to John relates several episodes that appear in none of the Synoptics. Even when John does cover the same ground, he sometimes takes a different angle of approach. He provides details that the others lack.

In terms of the chronology of Jesus' Passion, John

presents a major problem. He seems to contradict the timing that the other evangelists take for granted. Matthew, Mark, and Luke place the Last Supper squarely on Passover, the first night of the Feast of Unleavened Bread. John, however, clearly says that Jesus' condemnation took place on "the day of Preparation of the Passover" (John 19:14, 31). If Jesus died on the Day of Preparation, then the Romans executed his sentence at noon, "the sixth hour" (John 19:14), just as the Passover lambs were being sacrificed in the Temple. If John is correct, then it would seem that Jesus died several hours before the seder meals began in Jerusalem. If John is correct, then it would seem that Jesus could not have been in that upper room for the seder.

It would *seem* so. But things are not always as they seem.

What we know is that the early Christians were aware of the apparent discrepancy between these two accounts, and they kept both as they found them. A French scholar in the middle of the last century, Professor A. Jaubert, believed there were compelling reasons to accept *both* chronologies—the dates as we find them in the Synoptics *and* in John.[3] Her conclusions have been supported by the German exegete Eugen Ruckstuhl and, more recently, by James VanderKam of Notre Dame University.[4]

Jaubert used the recently discovered Dead Sea

Scrolls to demonstrate that Judaism was not monolithic in its religious observance in the first century. There were different sects and factions—Pharisees, Sadducees, Essenes, Zealots—and one way they differed from one another was in their timing of the feasts. The group that produced the Dead Sea Scrolls followed a solar calendar rather than the lunar calendar kept by the Jerusalem priests. For Jews following the solar calendar, in the year of Jesus' death Passover would have fallen on a Tuesday, while for the Temple priests it fell on the following Friday.

Jaubert noted, further, that the early Church commemorated the Last Supper not on the night before Good Friday but on the Tuesday before. This tradition is preserved in Syriac sources, including the third-century *Didascalia Apostolorum* (Teaching of the Apostles). Thus the early Christians whose language and culture were closest to Jesus' own—those who spoke and wrote in Aramaic—could have preserved the memory of a Tuesday Passover.

Jaubert's proposal solves not only the apparent discrepancy about the date of the Last Supper but also another problem in harmonizing the four Gospels: How could so many events have transpired between the evening meal on Thursday and the execution at midday on Friday? Christians since antiquity have struggled with that question. The Gospels report that Jesus underwent *five* trials, before *five* different judges (Annas, Caiaphas, Pilate, Herod, and the assembled Sanhedrin), in *five* different places—and all of this took place between the time of his arrest and the execution of his sentence. It's hard to see how so much could happen in those few hours after midnight. The events, as we find them, fit much more neatly into a Tuesday-to-Friday time frame: the Last Supper on Tuesday, the Jewish trials on Wednesday, the Roman trials on Thursday, and the death sentence and crucifixion on Friday.[5] That is, in fact, the sequence that appears in the *Didascalia Apostolorum*. (Pope Benedict XVI reproposed this chronology, persuasively, in his homily for the April 5, 2007, Mass of the Lord's Supper.)

PASCHAL WAGER

Research in areas like this leads us to be certain only of our uncertainty. It urges modesty, at least, as we draw conclusions. The confident assertion that three Gospels are wrong in their testimony seems unwarranted to me. Matthew, Mark, and Luke (the so-called Synoptic Gospels) state unequivocally that the Last Supper was a Passover meal. As a young pastor and scholar, I found no strong reasons to reject their claim. In thirty-five years of research since then, nothing new has emerged to change my mind.

As I was preparing those sermons in Fairfax, Virginia, I drew deeply from the work of Joachim Jeremias, a great Protestant exegete of the midcentury. He wrote a monumental study of the Last Supper and judged that it was quite likely a Passover meal. Helpfully, he summarized his findings in a list of fourteen ways that Jesus' meal with his disciples was consistent with a typical seder in antiquity.[6]

1. It happened in Jerusalem, where Jesus and the disciples were pilgrims.
2. It took place in a borrowed or rented room, the usual accommodation for Passover pilgrims.
3. It took place after sundown.
4. Jesus ate the meal, as a rabbi would, in the company of his disciples, numbering more than the ten required by custom.
5. The diners reclined as they ate. (Sitting was normal for nonfestive meals.)
6. They ritually purified themselves (by foot washing).
7. They broke bread, not just at the beginning of the meal but later in the meal as well (a custom peculiar to Passover).

8. They drank wine.

9. The wine was red.

10. The meal was prepared in haste.

11. They gave alms.

12. They sang a hymn.

13. Afterward they stayed in Jerusalem.

14. Jesus interpreted the symbolism of items on the menu.

It's a long list, and Jeremias defends every numbered item with scholarly rigor and abundant sources. The list alone takes up almost twenty pages in the book's third edition. It doesn't *prove* that the Last Supper was a seder—at least not to the satisfaction of some critical scholars. But it does show that the consistent claim of the three Synoptic Gospels is defensible and credible.

The Catholic Church has found it so. The *Catechism* states plainly the consensus of the ancient exegetical tradition: "By celebrating the Last Supper with his Apostles in the course of the Passover meal, Jesus gave the Jewish Passover its definitive meaning" (CCC, 1340). And, in his 2007 Apostolic Exhortation, *Sacramentum Caritatis*, Pope Benedict XVI spoke of "Jesus the true sacrificial lamb," whose "new and eternal covenant is the blood of the Lamb."[7] He continues by explaining that the institution of the Eucharist "took place within a ritual meal commemorating the foundational event of the people of Israel": the Passover. It "was a remembrance of the past, but at the same time a prophetic remembrance, the proclamation of a deliverance yet to come."[8]

NEW MOSES, NEW EXODUS

It was fitting, I believed, for the climax of redemption—the establishment of God's New Covenant—to begin at Passover. The Gospels themselves make the feast seem the proper (if not inevitable) setting. Passover is not a happenstance detail used to mark the date of a single incident. It is a recurring motif in the narrative of every Gospel.

It's the setting for many dramatic moments in Jesus' life. At Passover, when Jesus was twelve, he was separated from his parents and found after three days of searching (Luke 2:41–46)—a clear foreshadowing of his three days in the tomb. It was at Passover that Jesus cleansed the Temple (John 2:13–17), and at another Passover that he multiplied loaves and fishes and promised to provide the bread of life (John 6:4ff). Saint John's Gospel is structured with three Passover festivals as pillars, marking the years of Jesus' ministry (see John 2:13, 6:4, 11:55, and 13:1).

The Passover theme plays out in other ways. All the Gospels rather clearly portray Jesus as a new Moses

71

and his redemption as a new Exodus. The evangelists draw attention to the ways in which Jesus' life was similar to that of Moses. Both men were born in unusual circumstances—threatened by a murderous despot who commanded the slaughter of infants. When the family of Jesus took flight, they found refuge in Egypt; and the providential purpose of this was so that Jesus could retrace the steps of the Exodus. "This was to fulfill what the Lord had spoken by the prophet, 'Out of Egypt have I called my son'" (Matthew 2:15). Both Moses and Jesus fasted for forty days (see Exodus 34:28 and Matthew 4:2), and each delivered his particular "law" from a mount: for Moses, the Ten Commandments on Mount Sinai; for Jesus, the Sermon on the Mount. Jesus compared the loaves he multiplied to the manna given in the desert (John 6:49). Another mark of the Exodus is Jesus' evocation of Moses' lifting up of the bronze serpent and applying it to his own redemptive death (John 3:14).

Jesus implicitly compared himself to Moses as lawgiver (Mark 10:2–9) and as mediator. If Moses was the mediator of the Old Covenant, blessing the people with sacrificial blood, then Jesus is the mediator of the New Covenant, blessing with his own blood (Exodus 24:8, Matthew 26:28).

Saint Luke makes the connection between Jesus and Moses in a subtle but significant way as he describes Jesus' transfiguration. This passage marks, in fact, the only appearance of the Greek word *exodos* (Exodus) in the Gospels. Luke tells us that Jesus "appeared in glory" with Moses and Elijah "and spoke of his exodus, which he was to accomplish at Jerusalem" (Luke 9:31). The word *exodos* is variously translated into English as "departure" and "decease"; but the original Greek word is unusual, and the evangelist surely intended it to evoke the great event of Israelite history. In speaking of the "exodus" that Jesus was to "accomplish at Jerusalem," Luke was, I believe, setting the scene for Jesus' final Passover—the seder that he shared with his disciples, as it is recorded in the Gospels.

CHAPTER 6

Behold the Lamb

It's interesting that non-Christian commentators, in their study of the Last Supper, often note an "omission" that most Christians do not see. If this is Passover, they ask, where is the lamb? The lamb, after all, was the object most closely identified with Passover. In the New Testament books and the later rabbinic texts of the Talmud, the Greek word *Pascha* and the Hebrew word *Pesach* can indicate either the festal day or the sacrificial victim—or both.

To Christians, of course, Jesus is the definitive Lamb. He is the typological fulfillment of the original Passover lambs and all the lambs sacrificed afterward. Thus his presence obviates the need for any yearling sheep on the table.

But how do we know this? When—and why—did Christians begin to identify Jesus as the Lamb?

In pursuing an answer we see, again, the curious complementarity of the Synoptics on the one hand and John on the other. What is implicit in one is explicit in the other. Matthew, Mark, and Luke make no mention of a lamb. But John, who makes no mention of a Passover seder, repeatedly identifies Jesus as "the Lamb." The identification appears in other New Testament books as well—those that bear the names of Paul and Peter and John (again). But the best-known instance is at the beginning of John's Gospel. It is, in fact, the way John introduces Jesus to the reader.

The fourth Gospel begins with a theological statement about the eternal Word, the divine Son coeternal with the Father: "In the beginning was the Word, and the Word was with God, and the Word was God" (John 1:1). The Word then takes flesh and enters history as a man, recognized only by John the Baptizer, a prophet crying out in the Judean wilderness. The first time we see Jesus, he is walking toward this John, who says: "Behold, the Lamb of God, who takes away the sin of the world!" (John 1:29). A day later, John again sees Jesus and says: "Behold, the Lamb of God!" (John 1:36).

When Jesus was first recognized, then, he was seen as the Lamb of God. Jesus is the Lamb. After millennia of repetition—in Scripture, worship, and art—the phrase seems normal to us. But it must have seemed strange to John's hearers. Indeed, it must have seemed odd to all the generations that passed until Christianity was dominant in the world.

John's Jewish hearers would surely have made the connection with sacrifice. They were accustomed to the idea of a victim-lamb that takes away sins. But what could John mean by applying that title not to a small animal but to a grown man?

THE ROAST IS HISTORY

A prophet is someone who speaks for God. In the Old Testament, the prophets identified the signs of the times and pronounced God's judgment on events and people. Their oracles gave definitive meaning to the often-confusing news of the day. Sometimes, too, they predicted the future, foretelling the consequences of particular sins or virtuous acts.

Christian tradition places John the Baptizer within that category. He is a transitional figure: the last prophet of the Old Covenant, pointing the way to the New. When he declares that Jesus is the "Lamb of God," his meaning is obscure. But it has predictive and descriptive dimensions that become clear only when the story is fully told. The meaning becomes abundantly clear in light of Jesus' final Passover.

The Gospels tell us that John attracted great crowds of listeners. They included inquisitive priests and Levites (John 1:19) and Pharisees (John 1:24). What do you suppose they thought when John pointed to a man and called him God's Lamb?

Again, they could not help but make the association with Passover. A lamb that takes away sins is a sacrificial victim, and the lamb was identified most closely with Passover sacrifice. So they thought of the Passover lambs, and certainly this association engaged their imaginations. This was especially true for the priests and Levites who were present for the annual slaughter of a quarter million lambs at Passover. For them, John's imperative—"Behold the Lamb"—would evoke each victim as it was brought forward for sacrifice.

From the earliest rabbinic literature, we can perhaps learn something about what they saw every year at Passover—and what they imagined at the moment John issued his cry.

The Law prescribed that the Passover lamb was to be roasted whole, not boiled or cooked in parts. Later interpreters declared further that the lamb should not be roasted on metal spits. Why? Because any meat touching the metal would be *grilled* by the metal rather than *roasted* by the fire. For a similar reason, the interpreters prescribed that the spits should be made of pomegranate wood, which was extremely dry and so would not cause lamb flesh to be inadvertently steamed or boiled by trapped moisture.[1]

Writing in the second century, Saint Justin Martyr, a native of Palestine, described the preparation of the sacrifice, which was still offered by the Samaritans on Mount Gerizim in his day. He said that the animal was suspended by two wooden spits: one ran along the spine and the other across the back of the lamb.

> For the lamb, which is roasted, is roasted and dressed up in the form of the cross. For one spit is transfixed right through from the lower parts up to the head, and one across the back, to which are attached the legs of the lamb.[2]

That was the image of the lamb familiar to the priests and Levites—and indeed all the faithful Jews—among the crowds that gathered to hear John. They could not know the future when the Baptizer called it out, but Justin's hindsight was perfectly clear: "that lamb which was commanded to be wholly roasted was a symbol of the suffering of the cross which Christ would undergo."[3] More than a symbol, more than a shadow, it was a vivid image of the sacrifice to come.

The most extensive analysis of the cruciform lamb was published in *The Jewish Quarterly Review* in 1996. The author, Joseph Tabory of Israel's Bar-Ilan Univer-

sity, is a world-renowned Talmud scholar and Orthodox rabbi; and in his study he produced an exhaustive
analysis of the relevant literature. He notes that traditional Jewish practices help to explain even small
details of Christian iconography of the crucifixion. I
would add that they help us, at this remove, to "see"
for ourselves what arose in the imagination of John's
hearers.

Dr. Tabory invokes the authority of Rabbi Akiva,
whose life in Palestine stretched from the first century
to the second. Akiva reported that the animal's entrails
were removed before the sacrifice and wrapped, like
a helmet, around the head of the lamb. This custom
seems to be adapted from Exodus 12:9, which instructs
that the lamb should be "roasted, its head with its legs
and its inner parts." Dr. Tabory concludes:

> Perhaps there is a point of similarity between
> the lamb with its entrails around its head and
> Jesus' crown of thorns (Matt 27:29, Mk 15:17, Jn
> 19:2). . . . The similarity of the lamb helmeted
> in its entrails with the crowned Jesus may have
> served as additional evidence of the connection
> between the two.[4]

No one who heard John the Baptizer could have
predicted the ultimate fulfillment of his typology. But

some, perhaps beginning with the evangelist, lived to see it fulfilled. And they remembered.

PASCH'S PAST

I could not know quite so much in those years I was a young pastor in Virginia. Joseph Tabory's study did not appear till more than a decade later. But I was beginning to read more deeply in the early Fathers, and I was struck by Justin Martyr's testimony. It was compatible and indeed continuous with the testimony of the Bible.

The fourth Gospel calls Jesus the "Lamb of God, who takes away the sin of the world!" (John 1:29). The First Letter of Saint Peter confirms this when it says we are "ransomed . . . with the precious blood of Christ, like that of a lamb without blemish or spot" (1 Peter 1:18–19)—again invoking the Passover instructions of the Book of Exodus. And even though I was hardly a "hyper-typer," I had to follow the clear New Testament precedent of reading Isaiah's oracle as a prediction of Jesus: "like a lamb that is led to the slaughter, and like a sheep that before its shearers is dumb, so he opened not his mouth" (Isaiah 53:7; Acts 8:32). And finally there's the Book of Revelation, where the divine Son is called "the Lamb" twenty-eight times.

The New Testament overwhelmingly testifies that

Jesus is the Lamb of the New Covenant. The presence (or absence) of an unblemished infant sheep at the Last Supper is, in a sense, irrelevant. God's Lamb was there, and so the Passover obligation was fulfilled most perfectly and fittingly. The early Christian commentators agreed upon this, no matter how they approached differences between the Synoptics and John. They were not troubled at all by the absence of an animal from the narrative, because they saw that the Lord was there, and they saw that he said: "This is my body."

JUSTIN CASE

This is how I began to encounter the early Church Fathers: as exegetes—interpreters of the Bible. I had known their names, of course, because they were sometimes quoted in my seminary textbooks. Before these ventures in research, however, I had never bothered to spend much time searching out the context of those quotes.

Now I discovered that the Fathers were sensitive and careful readers of the Scriptures. They were not fanciful, as I had sometimes been led to believe. They cared deeply about historical accuracy. In fact, much of the historical record we have from the New Testament period, we have because the Fathers gathered it for us.

Witnesses like Justin Martyr were leading me, not away from the biblical text, but more deeply into it.

I found that others from the second century were occupied with the very matters that fascinated me in the twentieth century. Irenaeus of Lyons returned again and again to the theme of God's covenants, and he showed a similar interest in the Passover. And he, like Justin Martyr, enjoyed advantages that modern exegetes and theologians could never approximate. He received his training from Polycarp, who was a disciple of John the Evangelist. Justin grew up in Palestine at a time when the Temple was a living memory for some of his neighbors.

I was amazed. Then I discovered another of their contemporaries, Melito of Sardis. Melito was a bishop who died as an old man in A.D. 180. His city, today known as Sart in Turkey, had already been evangelized in the time of the Apostles, and its Christians were addressed directly in the Book of Revelation (see 3:1–4). Melito may have been a convert from Judaism. He had a profound grasp of the Old Testament, and he made pilgrimage at least once to the Holy Land. Although he was revered in the Church of the second century, only one of his works has survived to our day. It caught my eye because of its title: *Peri Pascha,* which is Greek for "On Passover."

Peri Pascha seems to be a long Easter sermon, perhaps preached through one of the all-night vigils observed by the ancient Church. Melito's discussion of the Exodus is rich, poetic, and imaginative, though he never strays from the facts. He wonders whether even the firstborn sons of Israel, all those years before, had been spared in anticipation of the blood of Jesus.

> Tell me, angel, what deterred you? The slaughter of the sheep or the life of the Lord? . . . You were deterred because you witnessed the mystery of the Lord accomplished in the sheep, the life of the Lord in the sacrifice of the sheep, the figure of the Lord in the death of the sheep.[5]

Melito had the goods. So many of the Fathers seemed to have the insight that I wanted. They even seemed to agree with me on practical particulars. They celebrated the Lord's Supper as their covenant renewal. They called it a memorial (*anamnesis*) and thanksgiving (*eucharistia*), thus placing it in the same categories as the Passover seder. What's more, they practiced it frequently—weekly or even daily, even in times of danger and persecution. I found evidence of frequent communion even in authors who predated Justin. It's there in Ignatius of Antioch, for example, a bishop who wrote in A.D. 107.

In this most primitive witness I found a certain

reassurance. Yet there was also a troubling element to their testimony. Why, for example, did these men—so steeped in the New Testament—insist on referring to the Lord's Supper as a sacrifice? The earliest witnesses, in fact, consistently called their worship *"the* sacrifice." The term made me uneasy. The New Testament teaches repeatedly that Jesus' death on the cross is the definitive sacrifice—"once for all." The Fathers, however, spoke as if each instance of the Lord's Supper was sacrificial.

Each instance reminded me of the warnings I'd received from members of my congregation who were former Catholics. They told me that the Catholic Church believed it was sacrificing Jesus, again and again, at every Mass. *That* idea was certainly contradictory to Scripture and an error I wanted to avoid at all costs. That desire pressed me on to deeper study of the Passover lamb, in both the Old Testament and the New.

CHAPTER 7

The Lamb from the Beginning

The Gospels, as I mentioned, are not the only books that refer to Jesus as the Lamb. The Book of Revelation makes the most of this imagery, in dozens of instances. Christ appears first, in clearly Paschal terms, as "a Lamb standing, as though it had been slain" (Revelation 5:6). Immediately that Lamb is worshipped as God by all the hosts of heaven. Angels and saints say with a loud voice: "Worthy is the Lamb who was slain, to receive power and wealth and wisdom and might and honor and glory and blessing!" (Revelation 5:12). The Lamb opens the seals of the previously inaccessible books. The people on earth "washed their robes and made them white in the blood of the Lamb" (Revelation 7:14). Later, the Seer evokes the Passover and Exodus again when he says that the victorious on the earth "have conquered . . . by the blood of the Lamb" (Revelation 12:11).

Then comes an enigmatic passage. It refers to the

heavenly record of those who are saved. The names of those who are saved are "written in the book of life of the Lamb slain from the foundation of the world" (Revelation 13:8). That's how the line appears in the King James Bible, which my senior pastor preferred.

I wondered what it could mean, and so I consulted the commentaries. They noted that more modern translators found the line inscrutable and so opted to "correct" the original. The Revised Standard Version, like most other recent English translations, shifted the phrase "from the foundation of the world" so that it clearly applies to "the book" rather than to the sacrifice of the Lamb. But that is not the sense of the Greek original, and commentaries will usually make note of this. Some commentators go so far as to protest the newer translations: "The Greek ... is clearly to be best rendered: 'slain since the foundation of the world.' This is what John means."[1]

The line seems to find echoes elsewhere in the New Testament. The First Letter of Peter begins with a chapter saturated with Passover imagery. The author reminds his readers that they have been "ransomed" by Christ's blood, "like that of a lamb without blemish or spot." Then, again comes the phrase: "He was destined before the foundation of the world but was made manifest at the end of the times for your sake" (1 Peter 1:18–20).

I puzzled over what these phrases could mean.

Christ died on a hill in Jerusalem around A.D. 30. How, then, could Scripture claim that he was slain "from the foundation of the world"?

Yet indeed it did. The Letter to the Hebrews further states that God's works "were *finished* from the foundation of the world" (Hebrews 4:3; emphasis added). The phrase appears again in Hebrews in the verse that assures us that Jesus' sacrifice was "once for all"—and it specifies that he did not have to "suffer repeatedly since the foundation of the world" (Hebrews 9:26).

Well, which should it be? How could he be sacrificed once in the first century and yet slain from the beginning?

READY, WILLING ABEL

The Letter to the Hebrews, which is much concerned with the history of sacrifice, finds Paschal hints even in the earliest human generations. Abel the herdsman sacrificed from the firstlings of his flock (see Genesis 4:4), and his offering was acceptable to God (Hebrews 11:4). Yet Abel himself was murdered by his brother, Cain, and the Letter goes on to compare that death with the sacrificial, saving death of Jesus (see Hebrews 12:24).

By the time of Jesus, this was likely already a traditional typological reading of the Torah. The rabbis of early Judaism taught that the events of the Book of Genesis foreshadowed the liberation to come in the Book of Exodus. What we see dimly, perhaps, in the story of Abel is clearer in the narrative of Abraham's offering of Isaac. Abraham's firstborn was redeemed when a ram suddenly appeared, caught in a thicket and ready to take Isaac's place—just as the Passover lamb would later take the place of Israel's firstborn. In the synagogues these stories were read from books called the Targums, Aramaic paraphrases of the biblical accounts that added details for clarity. According to the Targums, the ram seen by Abraham had been prepared *from the foundation of the world*.[2] In Jewish iconography, moreover, Abraham's ram is often portrayed as hanging from a tree, suggestive of the cruciform Passover lamb.[3]

The early Christians, in their turn, saw Christ preceded and prefigured in these Old Testament stories. Christ is, according to Melito of Sardis, "he who in Abel was slaughtered."[4]

> This is he who in Abel was slaughtered, in Jacob was exiled, in Joseph was sold, in Moses was exposed, in the lamb was immolated, in David was persecuted, in the prophets was maltreated. This is he . . . [who] on the cross was suspended, in the earth was buried, from the dead was resurrected, to the highest of heaven was lifted up.[5]

What do we see here? We see the victim Christ identified with the most vulnerable and persecuted people in all of history—even in the history that had preceded his earthly life. They, too, are "lambs slain" in a mysterious union with Jesus, ever since the beginning of the world.

The feasts of Passover and Unleavened Bread, as they were observed in Jesus' time, contained reminders of God's long-ago anticipation of salvation. At the time of the Exodus, the Law established the memorial as a festival lasting seven days. Seven (*sheva'* in Hebrew) was a significant number in Hebrew because it was associated with God's covenant (see Exodus 31:13–17). In the Book of Genesis, God creates the world in six days and seals his covenant with humanity on the seventh. Because of this, the Hebrew verb used for swearing a covenant oath is, literally translated, "to seven oneself." Philo of Alexandria, Jesus' Jewish contemporary, observed: "And, again, the feast is celebrated for seven days, on account of the honor due to that number, in order that nothing which tends to cheerfulness and to the giving of thanks to God may be separated from the holy number seven."[6]

The seven days of Passover were divinely intended to hark back to the foundation of the world. God wanted this feast to suggest a continuing process of renewal—creation and redemption—to be completed with Jesus in the fullness of time.

Melito compared the earlier events with an artist's model, fashioned in clay, whose true promise would be beautifully evident only in execution.

A PRIEST FOREVER

As a Calvinist, I was already convinced of the eternity of God's decrees. God is unchanging, and so his will has been fixed from the foundation of the world. But with these Scriptures I became increasingly aware of the ways God made his eternal, immutable will operative in time.

As I pondered these Scriptures, I began to glimpse the possibility of a different meaning of the phrase "once for all" when used to describe Jesus' sacrifice. I had formerly thought that "once for all" meant "over and done with." But now I began to see that "once for all" marked only the beginning. The Letter to the Hebrews makes this clear—in the very passage where it speaks of Jesus' "once for all" sacrifice.

It speaks of him as the definitive high priest entering the sanctuary of heaven. It compares and contrasts his sacrificial offering with those of the priests in the Jerusalem Temple. The earthly priests repeat their sacrifices of bulls and goats day after day. When they die, they are replaced by other priests.

Jesus, however, "holds his priesthood permanently, because he continues for ever" (Hebrews 7:24). Moreover, "He has no need, like those high priests, to offer sacrifices daily, first for his own sins and then for those of the people; he did this once for all when he offered up himself" (Hebrews 7:27).

Jesus' offering is his flesh, his body, which he bears into heaven and gives in love to the Father. His offering is never repeated because it never ceases. "He continues a priest forever" (Hebrews 7:3; see also Hebrews 7:17). So his priesthood never ends. He is always offering a sacrifice that is never repeated. I marveled at the strange beauty of God's plan.

WRATH OF THE LAMB

I also began to marvel at the strangeness of Our Lord's choice of his emblematic animal. Other symbols I could easily understand. In the Book of Revelation Jesus is also called the Lion of the tribe of Judah (Revelation 5:5). That made sense to me. Lions are powerful, like God. They command respect by their strength.

But a lamb? The pairing could not be more incongruous. Even adult sheep are remarkable only for their dullness and vulnerability. As babies they may be cute and cuddly and harmless—but do any of those qualities justify John's rhetoric in the Book of Revelation? In one passage he shows crowds of people fleeing "the wrath of the Lamb" (Revelation 6:16).

It should be comical. And it is if we allow ourselves the intellectual distance to ponder the incongruity. We may have to disengage ourselves from all the notions we've gained from centuries of art, hymns, and prayers—all of which exalt "the Lamb." We should think for a moment of the Gentile pagans who encountered phrases like "the wrath of the Lamb." Is such a phrase even credible? Think of its functional equivalents: "the wrath of the bunny" . . . "the wrath of the kitten" . . . "the wrath of the mouse"!

If we miss the paradox, we miss the point. Here, Jesus is bringing to fulfillment a principle that has been at work since the foundation of the world. We glimpse it in Abel and Isaac, who were vulnerable in their fidelity yet were vindicated. We see it symbolically in every Passover sacrifice.

The Lamb of the Book of Revelation, I realized, perfectly signifies a principle that Jesus himself elucidated for Saint Paul: "power is made perfect in weakness" (2 Corinthians 12:9). In the natural order, power and weakness stand as polar opposites. Yet in Christ the terms are somehow synonymous. Paul reflects upon the matter and concludes: "For he [Jesus] was crucified in weakness, but lives by the power of God" (2 Corinthians 13:4).

All the hideous, frightening beasts we encounter in the Book of Revelation, and all the kings and armies of the earth, must flee before the divine power manifest in the Lamb slain; for he is the fulfillment of the Passover. His blood is applied not to doorposts but to human bodies and souls, and it is victorious over every injustice, every sin, and even death.

The Lamb, moreover, willed to share his conquering power with those he redeemed from the human race. So, through his Passover, he makes them like himself—and then the mysteries and paradoxes abound. In Revelation 7:17, the Lamb becomes their shepherd! Like so much in the Book of Revelation, this seems to echo the doctrine of the Gospel of John, which begins with the identification of Jesus as "the Lamb" and ends with Jesus' identification of Christians as "my lambs" (John 21:15).

The Prophet Isaiah had foretold a God made visible, who would "feed his flock like a shepherd . . . [and] gather the lambs in his arms" (Isaiah 40:11). But God outperformed even those ancient oracles, as the Shepherd himself became a Lamb. He became like the flock, so that they might more easily love him and become like him.

This truth astonished the early Christians. The more

I contemplated the Passover, the more it astonished me. It was the power of God's saving covenant since the foundation of the world.

I was beginning to reconsider when it was begun. This would definitely affect my understanding of my pastor's question from years before. It would affect my understanding of Jesus' Passover, with the Lamb and the cups. It affected my understanding of when and how and why "It is finished."

CHAPTER 8

Unleavened Bread

I had studied theology at two respected institutions. I had been ordained for ministry, and soon I was also teaching theology to Presbyterian seminarians. In 1982 and 1983 I served as assistant professor at Dominion Theological Institute in McLean, Virginia, not far from my church. As a student and teacher of theology—and indeed as a Christian—I knew that Christ stood at the center of history, creation, and redemption. Saint Paul put it well: "for in him all things were created, in heaven and on earth, visible and invisible . . . all things were created through him and for him. He is before all things, and in him all things hold together" (Colossians 1:16–17).

What I was beginning to see, in my deepening study of the Passover, was how Christ stood *eternally* as the Passover lamb. This image—prominent in the Gospels and prevalent in the Book of Revelation—was not simply his identity ever after the cross. It was not a name he assumed with his public ministry or with his death. It was not something he picked up during his incarnational sojourn. The "Lamb slain" is a name that suited him "from the foundation of the world." It is a name and an identity that somehow transcended time.

Jesus was the Lamb. Jesus is the Lamb. So I was not scandalized, as some readers are, that the Gospel narratives never mention the presence of a lamb at the Last Supper. If there was a lamb, it was incidental, not worth mentioning. At most, the sacrificial lamb was the diminishing shadow of the true Lamb.

The true Lamb would become the once-for-all sacrifice, and Jesus seemed to foretell this at his seder. He did so, however, in terms that must have seemed strange. He identified himself not with the sacrificial lamb at the seder but rather with the unleavened bread.

> And he took bread, and when he had given thanks he broke it and gave it to them, saying, "This is my body which is given for you. Do this in remembrance of me." (Luke 22:19)

And so Christians have done ever since. Our Presbyterian church scheduled the Lord's Supper infrequently, but whenever we did, we observed it with bread. I wondered, now, at the meaning of the bread that Jesus had at hand that evening.

EAT THE FLESH

The biblical ordinance for Passover was clear in the Book of Exodus. The essential menu was set. "They shall eat the flesh that night, roasted; with unleavened bread and bitter herbs they shall eat it" (Exodus 12:8). From that single verse Rabban Gamaliel drew his list of three items that must be present on the table and explained to all present.

The lamb was consumed in a day, but unleavened bread was to be a hallmark of the entire week that followed.

> Seven days you shall eat unleavened bread; on the first day you shall put away leaven out of your houses, for if any one eats what is leavened, from the first day until the seventh day, that person shall be cut off from Israel. (Exodus 12:15)

Passover began the weeklong festival of Unleavened Bread. Jews treated the two feasts, Passover and

Unleavened Bread, as a unit. The historian Josephus used the terms interchangeably and synonymously.[1]

The bread was important, and its meaning complex. The original command suggests that the bread was to be unleavened because the Israelites were in a hurry to leave Egypt. They had no time to let dough rise: "it was not leavened, because they were thrust out of Egypt and could not tarry" (Exodus 12:39). Matzo, moreover, would be easier for the travelers to store and carry—and less likely to spoil during their journey.

Those are good, practical reasons for ancient travelers to make their bread without leaven. Later Jewish commentators suggested other reasons why matzo was especially fitting for the occasion. Philo of Alexandria noted that Passover always falls in early spring, before the grain is fully grown. Thus the bread is imperfect because it belongs to the future. The bread itself points forward in hope.

Philo noted also that unleavened bread is just ground wheat and water. Thus it is a pure gift from God, whereas leavened bread requires human art and planning. The unleavened bread, then, represents the gratuitousness of God's act of redemption as a new creation (symbolized by the seven days of the feast).[2]

The Law was insistent that the Passover bread must be unleavened. The penalty for using anything else was most severe: "if any one eats what is leavened, from the first day until the seventh day, that person shall be cut off from Israel" (Exodus 12:15). Unleavened bread was an essential sign in the Passover rite. There was nothing optional about it. To eliminate it or substitute for it was to bring a curse upon oneself.

Although it was integral to a festive occasion, matzo was called "the bread of affliction" (Deuteronomy 16:3), because it was Israel's sustenance in their hour of flight.

Before the time of the Exodus, there is only one mention of unleavened bread in the Torah, and it has always seemed significant to me. It is in the story of the destruction of Sodom. As the destroying angels make their way toward the city, the patriarch Lot delays their mission by showing them hospitality. He invited them into his home, "and he made them a feast, and baked unleavened bread, and they ate" (Genesis 19:3). The meal has suggestive similarities with the much later Passover. When the Destroyer came to Egypt, he spared the houses of the Israelites—the houses where the families were eating unleavened bread.

There was much, then, that could be said about the meaning of the unleavened bread during the seder meal. Yet Jesus said none of this. Instead, he took the bread, broke it, and gave it a new meaning. He said: "This is my body." And then he issued the command for his disciples to "do this" as his memorial.

With those actions and words he changed the

character of the Passover forever. In none of the chapters of the Acts of the Apostles will you see Christians sitting down to a Passover seder and eating lamb. What do you see instead? You find them "breaking bread" (Acts 2:46; see also 20:7). Jesus had told them, "do this in remembrance of me," and this is what they did, not annually, not quarterly, but rather frequently. It was, in fact, the early Christians' most characteristic act. "And they devoted themselves to the apostles' teaching and fellowship, to the breaking of bread and the prayers" (Acts 2:42).

THE PAUSE THAT RE-FLESHES

I was simultaneously excited and frightened by the discoveries I made in my studies. I felt conscience-bound to follow where the Scriptures led me, and I couldn't help but apply what I learned to my church's practice of worship. When I did so, however, members of the congregation would observe: "That looks Catholic!" Some of them liked the changes, and some didn't, but their observation was consistent. What we were doing "looked Catholic."

Around this time, I was teaching the Gospel of John to seminarians at Dominion. Since John structured his narrative around three Passovers, I found myself further immersed in the study of Jewish ritual and Christian sacraments. I had read John's Gospel dozens of times by then, but never before had I been so struck by its Passover character. And I couldn't help but relate John's famous Bread of Life Discourse to the enigmatic meaning that Jesus gave to the bread at the Last Supper. He said, "This is my body," and he offered no explanation. But, according to John, he had already given the explanation:

> Jesus said to them, "I am the bread of life; he who comes to me shall not hunger, and he who believes in me shall never thirst. . . . I am the living bread which came down from heaven; if any one eats of this bread, he will live for ever; and the bread which I shall give for the life of the world is my flesh." (John 6:35, 51)

We're told that the crowd who heard these words could not bear what Jesus was telling them. They gave him every opportunity to explain it away as a metaphor or a symbol; but he answered them in increasingly graphic terms, promising them "bread" that was his "flesh." In the end, we're told, "many of his disciples drew back and no longer went about with him" (John 6:66). They said: "This is a hard saying; who can listen to it?" (6:60).

John tells us that the occasion for the discourse was the Passover (6:4). In the discourse, Jesus identified himself as the "true bread from heaven" (6:32) and the "bread of life" (6:35), drawing a parallel with Moses, through whom God fed manna to the Israelites (Exodus 16:4ff.).

As we discussed the passage in class, the students grew excited. It was obviously new material for many of them. The passage is certainly downplayed or avoided outright by evangelicals—in spite of its great length and its dire terms, in spite of its important messages about discipleship and authority. Now, years later, I can see why we avoided it. It *is* a hard saying—and it was especially hard to square with the practice of worship in our churches.

My students eagerly took up the discussion of the Bread of Life Discourse in light of the Synoptics' account of the Last Supper. Then we considered both in light of the Old Testament's doctrine of sacrifice. This was immediately relevant; because it was not enough for the Israelites in Egypt to *kill* the lamb. Death was only one aspect of the sacrifice. The ultimate goal was restoring communion between God and his people, which was ritually accomplished by the Passover meal. In other words, the Chosen People *had to eat the lamb.* Jesus, whom John had identified as the "Lamb of God," was indeed telling his chosen disciples a hard saying: that his flesh would be their bread, and their salvation would depend upon the consumption of that flesh.

What's more, it was not a once-and-done event. He commanded his disciples to "do this" ever afterward as his memorial sacrifice. His ultimate goal was to restore communion, which he accomplished by means of the bread that was his body. The conclusion seemed inevitable to me: we, too, have to eat the Lamb.

The students, some of whom knew more about Catholicism than I did, began to echo what the people in my congregation had been saying: "This sounds so Catholic." It alarmed me, and eventually it caused me to question my commitment to the authority and tradition of my denomination. My Calvinist teachers had instilled in me a profound reverence for Scripture. They had taught me that the words of the Bible were inspired and inerrant. But what if I found the words of the Bible to contradict the practice and doctrine of our Calvinist churches?

I did not think the Catholic Church could be the true Church. I "knew," after all, that Catholicism was rife with obvious errors. Catholics believed that they sacrificed Jesus repeatedly—killing him again and again every time they celebrated the Mass. I wasn't so much tempted to believe that they could be right. But what if *we* were wrong? And what if we were *very* wrong about something so important as the renewal of the New Covenant in Jesus Christ?

Saint Paul's admonition took on a powerful meaning in this light: "Christ, our paschal lamb, has been sacrificed" (1 Corinthians 5:7). Notice that he did not conclude, "It's once for all! So there is nothing more to be done!" Instead, he says in the very next verse, "Let us, therefore, celebrate the festival, not with the old leaven, the leaven of malice and evil, but with the unleavened bread of sincerity and truth" (1 Corinthians 5:8). In other words, something more remains for us to do. We are to feast upon Jesus, the Bread of Life and our Passover lamb.

Like Jesus before him, Paul did not allow his hearers to mistake his meaning. He left no room for merely symbolic interpretation. Instead he reinforced the flesh-and-blood realism of sacramental communion. In the same Letter to the Corinthians he wrote: "The bread which we break, is it not a participation [Greek *koinonia*] in the body of Christ?" (1 Corinthians 10:16). And later he warned that "anyone who eats and drinks without discerning the body eats and drinks judgment upon himself" (1 Corinthians 11:29).

The terms here, as in the Bread of Life Discourse, are rather dire. I was deeply grateful to God for what he was showing me, but I was also deeply troubled. Jesus' gift to us was so great. Yet were we truly "discerning it"? Or were we eating and drinking judgment upon ourselves?

I had no clear answer. But I knew that I could not, in good conscience, continue doing what I was doing. I could not present myself as a pastor of the Orthodox Presbyterian Church and a teacher of its doctrine. The prospect was frightening to me. My degrees had prepared me for no other employment, and I was now a husband and father. But I could see no other path.

Into this mix of emotions came heartbreakingly good news. Dominion Theological Institute offered me my dream job. The administration asked if I would accept the position of academic dean for the seminary. I had been praying for this moment. I had been dreaming of this moment. And yet I knew that I would have to refuse the offer.

For Israel, the bread from heaven was also the bread of affliction. The connection was not lost on me. With my family I began my own exodus. We returned to western Pennsylvania, where Kimberly and I had spent our growing-up years; and there I took a position as assistant to the president at Grove City College, our alma mater. The job would be less demanding than a pastorate. It would leave me time for focused study and prayer.

CHAPTER 9

The Cups

I found solace in study. I found answers, too—and I turned up more questions. The scholars I consulted raised still more questions.

Among the difficulties presented by the Last Supper narratives is the way they end the seder prematurely, leaving the liturgy unfinished. Jesus and his disciples exit the room and go off into the night singing a hymn (see Mark 14:26). But they neglect to drink the cup of wine prescribed to accompany the hymn—the fourth cup. This is a glaring omission.

Indeed, Jesus draws attention to the omission and signals that it is intentional. As he takes the third cup he says: "Truly, I say to you, I shall not drink again of the fruit of the vine until that day when I drink it new in the kingdom of God" (Mark 14:25).

The problem arises often in the works of Jewish scholars. For them, the Gospels provide a potentially valuable early witness to the observance of Passover, so they submit them to close analysis. The missing final cup presents a serious problem.

As a pastor—even a pastor of a traditionally non-liturgical church—I knew what happened whenever I violated people's expectations at Sunday worship. If you skip the customary hymn, there's an outcry. Everyone notices. Many complain. In a first-century Jewish milieu, with its tightly prescribed rituals, the absence would be far more shocking—especially if a rabbi chose to stop *just short* of the climactic moment of the most essential liturgy on the most important feast of the year. Even twenty centuries later, the omission remains a scandal to readers who have lovingly observed the seder throughout their lives.

But Jesus did skip the fourth cup. He said out loud that he was doing so. He offered no explanation.

THE GREAT OMISSION

Let's look at the cup in context. At first glance the wine might not seem as essential to the seder as, say, the lamb or the unleavened bread. It does not appear at all in the rubrics prescribed by the Torah. Historians believe the four cups of wine were added later to heighten the banquet's sense of festivity—"wine to gladden the heart of man" (Psalm 104:15). Rabban Gamaliel does not number wine among the three essential elements of the Passover; but the Mishnah nonetheless carefully prescribes the dispensation of the drinks.

The Passover meal was divided into four parts, or courses, and each was accompanied by a cup of red wine mixed with water. The poorest Jews were guaranteed four cups at the community's expense, so that their experience of the festival should be complete. The rabbis' instructions governed even the proportion of wine to water in each cup.

As we've seen, the meal's first course consisted of a special blessing (*kiddush*) spoken over the first cup of wine, followed by the serving of a dish of herbs.

The second course included a recital of the Passover narrative, the questions and answers, and the "Little Hallel" (Psalm 113), followed by the drinking of the second cup of wine.

The third course was the main meal, consisting of lamb and unleavened bread, after which was drunk the third cup of wine, known as the "cup of blessing."

The culmination of the seder was the singing of the "Great Hallel" (Psalms 114–118) and the drinking of the fourth cup of wine, often called the "cup of consummation."

Historians of the Passover see this pattern reflected in the Gospel narratives of the Last Supper. The twentieth century's most respected scholar of ancient Jewish law, Rabbi David Daube of Oxford, considered the Gospel sequence in a study titled (spoiler alert) "The Omission of the Fourth Cup." He notes that the cup Jesus pronounced to be the "blood of the covenant" (Mark 14:24) is clearly the third cup of the haggadah, which was known as the "blessing cup" because it was consumed with the prayer of thanksgiving at the main course. Saint Paul seems to confirm this cup as the third in his own discussion of the Lord's Supper: "The cup of blessing which we bless, is it not a participation in the blood of Christ?" (1 Corinthians 10:16).

With the prayer over that cup, Jesus tells his disciples he will "not drink again of the fruit of the vine until . . . I drink it new in the kingdom of God." David Daube observes: "The meaning is that the fourth cup will not be taken, as would be the normal thing, at a subsequent stage of the service; it will be postponed till the kingdom is fully established."[1]

In its immediate context, the fourth cup loomed large. It brought closure to the rites that renewed Israel's covenant with God. Its omission would be like a blank spot on a wall in the Louvre—in the place of the *Mona Lisa*. After moving in line for hours, people expect to arrive at their promised (and, in this case, accustomed) destination. The omission of the fourth cup—the "cup of consummation"—would have been jarring. It would, indeed, change the disciples' sense of all that had gone before.[2]

CUPS AND DOWNS

In the Scriptures, a cup of wine is rarely (if ever) simply a cup of wine. The "cup" is one of the most significant and suggestive objects in Hebrew literature. Its symbolic value is complex. It represents the future. It represents judgment. It represents blessing. It represents wrath. It represents joy. It represents sorrow. And it can signify all of these things at the same time.

Every cup of wine is consequential, determinative of life to come. It is the mark of righteousness, then, to choose the Lord as one's "cup." The Psalmist proclaims: "The LORD is my chosen portion and my cup; you hold my lot" (Psalm 16:5). And elsewhere, similarly: "I will lift up the cup of salvation and call on the name of the LORD" (Psalm 116:13). The cup is a characteristic element in Israel's worship. It signifies an acceptance, in advance, of God's providential care.

The future remains, however, a matter of uncertainty and anxiety. The constant message of the Bible is that we should entrust everything to the Lord. But people have always been tempted to hedge their bets. The Prophet Isaiah railed against his contemporaries who forgot the

God of Israel and rather sought their future with idols, filling "cups of mixed wine for Destiny" (Isaiah 65:11). In doing so, they broke their covenant with the true God and established a bond instead with Fortune and Destiny, the at best illusory (or at worst demonic) idols of their pagan neighbors.

The cup is, in either case, a sign of a shared life. It signifies a covenant bond, a family bond. The prophets speak of God's relationship with Israel in such terms, comparing it to a marriage (see, for example, Hosea 2:18–20; Jeremiah 2:2, 3:1). Acts of idolatry were also considered in such terms, but rather as adulterous unions. The word used to describe the false gods, *ba'al*, derives from a common Semitic word for husband (Hosea 2:16–17). To worship falsely was to enter into an illicit relationship. To fill a cup with wine for an idol was symbolic of the treachery—giving to a false god what belonged to the true.

What people found fearful about true worship was often their own unworthiness. Every covenant, as I've pointed out, promises either blessings or curses— blessings upon faithful fulfillment, curses upon infidelity. Everyone who enters the covenant drinks from the same cup, but the meaning of the cup depends on their faithfulness. They drink it either to salvation or to condemnation.

Thus we find the covenantal cup called "the cup of

salvation," as just described, but also the "cup of his wrath" (see Isaiah 51:17). The cup of blessing overflows to the righteous (Psalm 23:5). The cup of wrath overflows to the wicked:

> *Woe to him who makes his neighbors drink*
> > *of the cup of his wrath, and makes them drunk,*
> > *to gaze on their shame!*
> *You will be sated with contempt instead of glory.*
> *Drink, yourself, and stagger!*
> *The cup in the LORD's right hand*
> > *will come around to you,*
> > *and shame will come upon your glory!*
> > > (Habbakuk 2:15–16)

This sense of "the cup" is not peculiar to the Old Testament. Saint Paul uses similar terms to discuss the chalice of the Lord's Supper—the third cup, the blessing cup, which Jesus consecrated. He tells the Corinthians:

> The cup of blessing which we bless, is it not a participation in the blood of Christ? The bread which we break, is it not a participation in the body of Christ? . . . You cannot drink the cup of the Lord and the cup of demons. You cannot partake of the table of the Lord and the table of demons. (1 Corinthians 10:16, 21)

Yet, again, even for Christians, the "cup of blessing" can also be a cup of severe judgment and wrath. To those who approach unworthily it merits not the blessing of the covenant but the curse. Thus, Paul warns the same congregation:

> Let a man examine himself, and so eat of the bread and drink of the cup. For any one who eats and drinks without discerning the body eats and drinks judgment upon himself. That is why many of you are weak and ill, and some have died. (1 Corinthians 11:28–30)

In the New Testament, God's covenant is still signified by the cup—and the terms remain the same. "I have set before you life and death, blessing and curse" (Deuteronomy 30:19). The cup represents the future: blessed or cursed.

CROSS PURPOSES

A cup in any Jewish liturgy was an item of consequence. A cup in the seder was supremely important. What then are we to make of Jesus' omission of the final cup of his last Passover?

Some scholars speculate that psychological factors

account for Jesus' forgetfulness. They point out how, subsequently, he "began to be greatly distressed and troubled. And he said to them, 'My soul is very sorrowful, even to death'" (Mark 14:33–34). Perhaps he was too upset to be bothered with liturgical precision in following the rubrics.

While that analysis may seem plausible, further reflection renders it unlikely. For one thing, if he was so distracted and confused, it seems doubtful Jesus would forget and interrupt the Passover liturgy *after expressly declaring his intention not to drink the fourth cup*, especially since he went ahead and sang the Great Hallel. Why would he declare himself so plainly before acting in so disorderly a fashion? His other actions that night indicate a man admittedly distressed, but in full possession of himself. Why then did he choose not to drink?

I looked to the next point on the Gospel time line, and that was Jesus' prayer in the Garden of Gethsemane. There I found what I was looking for. I found at least a reference to the missing cup. "And going a little farther he fell on his face and prayed, 'My Father, if it be possible, *let this cup pass from me*; nevertheless, not as I will, but as thou wilt'" (Matthew 26:39).

This cup! Three times Jesus prayed for his Father to take away "this cup." An obvious question arises: *What* cup was Jesus talking about?

Some scholars explain Jesus' language by identifying

it with "the cup of God's wrath" in the Old Testament prophets (Isaiah 51:17; Jeremiah 25:15). Surely there is a connection here, but the connection seems less direct than does the primary link suggested by the Passover setting.

Note how Jesus' resolution not to drink "the fruit of the vine" seems to reappear in the scene at Golgotha right before he is crucified: "And they offered him wine mingled with myrrh; but he did not take it" (Mark 15:23). The narrative does not explain his refusal, but it probably points back to Jesus' pledge not to drink until his kingdom is manifested in glory.

Then the plot takes an interesting turn. "After this Jesus, knowing that all was now finished, said (to fulfill the Scripture), 'I thirst' " (John 19:28).

Jesus was thirsty long before this closing moment of his life. His words, therefore, must reflect more than a desire for a last bit of fluid. He seems to have been in full possession of himself as he realized that "all was now finished."

Whatever it is that was now finished seems to be directly connected to his utterance, which he spoke "to fulfill the Scripture." More things fall into place upon reading what followed his expression of thirst: "A bowl full of vinegar stood there; so they put a sponge full of the vinegar on hyssop and held it to his mouth" (19:29). Only John noticed that hyssop, the branch prescribed in the Passover law for sprinkling the blood of the lamb, was used (Exodus 12:22).

This verse reveals something very significant. Jesus had left unfinished the Passover liturgy when he chose to omit the fourth cup. He had stated his intention not to drink wine again until he came into the glory of his kingdom. Then he *refused* wine offered to him on one occasion, right before being nailed to the cross (Mark 15:23). Finally, at the very end, Jesus was offered "sour wine" or "vinegar" (John 19:30; Matthew 27:48; Mark 15:36; Luke 23:36). All the Synoptics testify to this. But only John tells us how he responded: "When Jesus had received the sour wine, he said, 'It is finished'; and he bowed his head and gave up his spirit" (19:30).

It is finished! At last I had an answer to the preacher's question. It was the Passover that was now finished!

Nothing, it seems, was missing from his seder. All was consummated, completed, brought to conclusion with the wine the Lord consumed with his final breath.

CHAPTER 10

The Hour

I returned often in those days to the Gospel According to John—that most Paschal of the Gospels. When a group of students invited me to speak at Grove City College, I knew what topic I wanted to address.

I was now reading all the pages of John's Gospel in light of the last pages—the consummation of Jesus' life on the cross. As I've already mentioned, the Passover is profoundly important in the fourth Gospel. The narrative is structured around three celebrations of the feast. Jesus is identified repeatedly in the first chapter as the "Lamb of God."

Yet John remains unique among the Gospels because he does not explicitly present the Last Supper as a Passover seder. In Luke's Gospel, Jesus expresses his passionate desire to eat this Passover with his disciples. In Matthew and Mark he repeatedly speaks of the meal as the Passover. In the Synoptics, moreover, the center-piece of the Last Supper is the institution narrative—the account of Jesus' establishment of the Lord's Supper. These passages present difficulties, but the difficulties are not insurmountable.

First, the Last Supper described in John 13 does not mention the cups of wine or the broken bread, but it does show several other characteristics that, taken together, suggest that it was a Passover seder. Chapter 13 begins by setting the scene "before the feast of Passover"—that is, on the afternoon before the seder. The meal that follows takes place at night (John 13:30); the diners are reclined at the table (John 13:23); morsels of food are "dipped" before being eaten (John 13:26); and some of the disciples assumed that Judas was leaving to make an offering to the poor (John 13:29). While there is no overt mention of the Passover feast, all of these details describe actions that were customary for the seder, prescribed by both Scripture and rabbinic tradition.

John's description of the crucifixion is similarly filled with Paschal imagery. All of the Gospels note that Jesus is offered wine (or vinegar) to drink as he suffers, but only John mentions that the sponge is born aloft by a hyssop branch (John 19:29). Hyssop was the plant used by the Israelites, at the first Passover, to smear the lamb's blood on their doorposts (Exodus 12:21–23). Only John notes that Jesus is wearing a seamless garment—a typical priestly vestment (John 19:23), that his death took place at the usual hour of sacrifice in the Temple, and that none of Jesus' bones were broken (John 19:33–36)—a requirement of the Paschal lamb. Thus, in John's Gospel, Jesus appears everywhere as the perfect fulfillment of the Passover. He is the high priest, and he is the sacrificial lamb.

Finally, John seems to assume that his readers already know the accounts of Jesus' Passion in the Synoptic Gospels. The other three Gospels establish that Jesus, at the Last Supper, deferred the final cup at the meal. As he did so, he plainly stated his intention: "I tell you I shall not drink again of this fruit of the vine until that day when I drink it new with you in my Father's kingdom" (Matthew 26:29; see also Mark 14:25 and Luke 22:18).

The Synoptics raise the problem of the missing fourth cup, but they don't resolve the problem. If all we had were Matthew, Mark, and Luke, we might conclude that Jesus was deferring the fourth cup until the time of his Second Coming. But John completes, supplements, and illuminates the Synoptics.

John explains the meaning of Jesus' deferral. John assumes that readers know the Synoptics—that they know what happened in the upper room and they know what Jesus prayed in the Garden. But John connects the dots for us. Although he does not tell us the words or themes of Jesus' prayer in Gethsemane, he is the only evangelist who informs us of Jesus' words to Peter: "Put your sword into its sheath; shall I not drink the cup which the Father has given me?" (John 18:11). The mention of "the cup" would make no sense if the reader was unaware of the Synoptic tradition.[1]

All four Gospels tell us that Jesus was offered a drink of sour wine at his place of execution; but Matthew, Mark, and Luke don't say whether Jesus drank the wine. How do we know, then, whether he drank the wine? How do we know that Jesus' reference to drinking wine in "the kingdom" does not refer to his Second Coming at the end of time?

Because John, who provides the only eyewitness account of the event, assures us that Jesus drank the wine (John 19:29–30). John reveals, then, that the kingdom is not what many people had imagined it would be. The nature of the kingdom is divine love given freely and completely—and manifest upon the cross (see John 12:31–33).

YOURS, MINE, AND HOURS

As I continued my studies in John, I discovered many ways that Jesus was preparing his disciples, all along, for what they would endure at the end. I noticed that Jesus referred often to the moment when his mission would be fulfilled, and he called it his "hour." I read works by Augustine, the great Scripture scholar of the fourth and fifth centuries, and I learned that he held the terms "hour" and "cup" to be synonymous in John's Gospel—"the hour of his Passion, which he also expresses presently by the term *cup*."[2]

John's idea of "the hour," I came to see, would be key to my understanding of the Passover and the cup. I took up the matter in my sessions with my very precocious group of college kids.

The word "hour"—in Greek, *hora*—has a specific literal sense in the Gospel. For John and for Jesus, the word denotes the culminating moment of Jesus' life and mission, the historic events of his sacrificial self-offering. "So they sought to arrest him; but no one laid hands on him, because *his hour* had not yet come" (John 7:30). "He taught in the temple; but no one arrested him, because *his hour* had not yet come" (John 8:20).

The references to Jesus' arrest make it obvious when his "hour" would come at last. It would come in the final days of his earthly life, with his suffering, death, and resurrection. But it would involve much more. As I looked at the fourth Gospel in its entirety, and searched out all the references to Jesus' "hour," I discovered a still-deeper *spiritual sense* to the word. Taken together, all the "hours" of John's Gospel point to a time that began all those centuries ago in a city in Palestine; but they point also, quite clearly and specifically, to a time and a place that Christians should still know today.

ALONG COMES MARY

Jesus could have chosen another word. In Aramaic and Greek, as in modern English, options abound. He could have spoken of his "moment," his "day," or his "time." But he chose "hour," and he used that word in a way that is remarkably consistent—and with a powerful cumulative effect.

Jesus used the word "hour" to speak about the central mystery of faith, the work he had come to accomplish. His first recorded use of the word is on the day of his first miracle, the wedding feast at Cana in Galilee. He arrives at the feast that Sunday along with his mother and his disciples. Soon afterward, the party runs out of wine—an embarrassing situation for the newlyweds— and Mary says to her son, "They have no wine" (John 2:3). Jesus replies: "O woman, what have you to do with me? *My hour* has not yet come" (John 2:4).

Does his response strike you as odd? Mary had made a simple, empirical observation—the wine had run out. But Jesus appears to read far too much into it. His response—"O woman, what have you to do with me? My hour has not yet come"—seems way out of proportion to Mary's report. But maybe not.

To make sense of Jesus' assertion "My hour has not yet come," we must identify the underlying assumption. Clearly, he anticipates an "hour" when something momentous will happen. Yet that time is not now. We can compare it to an engaged man inviting his fiancée to his bedroom to see his etchings. The fiancée would be right to respond: "What are you saying? Our hour has not yet come." Again, the assumption is that the hour will one day be here—when it will be proper for them to enter his bedroom—but not yet.

But what was the assumption underlying the conversation at Cana? What could possibly have reminded Jesus of his "hour"? What in his mother's request even remotely suggests the still-distant time of Jesus' self-offering? Let's look at the rest of the scene, to see if we can search out some detail that the wedding feast had in common with the hour of Jesus' Passion, death, and resurrection.

Mary's request had an amazing effect on her son. "Now six stone jars were standing there, . . . each holding twenty or thirty gallons. Jesus said, . . . 'Fill the jars with water.' And they filled them up to the brim. He said to them, 'Now draw some out, and take it to the steward of the feast.' . . . When the steward of the feast tasted the water now become wine, . . . [he] called the bridegroom and said to him, 'Every man serves the good wine first; and when men have drunk freely, then the poor wine; but you have kept the good wine until now'" (John 2:6–10).

What does this story tell us about Jesus' hour? Cana, we are told, was the first of Jesus' "signs." John uses the word "sign" instead of "wonder" or "miracle," because he wishes to highlight the symbolic meaning behind the miracles. A sign is a miracle, yes, but also a harbinger of something greater.

Look back through the exchange between Jesus and his mother. Only one thing in Mary's request could have triggered such a response: "They have no wine."

Jesus knew that when his hour did arrive, he would provide wine, indeed the finest of wine. But that definitive hour had not yet come.

SAMARITAN GOODS

Let's move on to the next instance of the "hour." In chapter 4 of John's Gospel, Jesus is speaking with a person who today might be called "marginalized." She was a Samaritan, a member of a rebel people who, though they were descended from Israel, had for centuries observed a degraded and idolatrous religion. Devout Jews did not stoop to speak with Samaritans. Yet Jesus chose this Samaritan woman to receive the first explicit teaching about his "hour." After she speaks of the religious differences between Jews and Samaritans, he replies: "Woman, believe me, *the hour* is coming when neither on this mountain nor in Jerusalem will you worship the Father. . . . The *hour* is coming, and now is, when the true worshipers will worship the Father in spirit and truth" (John 4:21–23).

Once more, we find him speaking of his hour, but again it goes beyond the historic events surrounding his Passion. At Cana, his words revealed that he expected to provide wine when the hour came. Now, with the Samaritan woman, he reveals another dimension.

In this passage, we learn that his hour is not only a time of providing wine. It is even more a time of worship—a radically new way of worship, which even the Jews in the Jerusalem Temple had never known. When the hour comes, the living water of the Holy Spirit will be poured out to enable all people to worship "in spirit."

That outpouring changed everything. Now, in Jesus' hour, it's not *where* you worship that's important but *how* you worship. Nor is worship restricted to the Chosen People or the Jerusalem Temple. Worship "in spirit" is available even to those people whom the Jews had considered spiritually dead. But how can this be? The answer, again, is in the hour.

GREEKS BARING GIFTS

Jesus returned to the theme of his hour in the fifth chapter of John, as he explained to people why he was healing on the Sabbath. He told the crowd: "Truly, truly, I say to you, *the hour* is coming, and now is, when the dead will hear the voice of the Son of God, and those who hear will live" (John 5:25–29).

Here is a third dimension of the hour. Not only is it a time of worship when the "best wine" will be provided, but it is also a time when the Word of God will bring people to repentance and forgiveness—in short, to new life.

Jesus' next discussion of his hour takes place at Passover (John 12:20ff). In Jerusalem, some Greeks approach Philip and request an audience with Jesus. Philip and Andrew inform Jesus, perhaps expecting him to say, "Send them in." But, as at Cana, Jesus responds in a way that is unexpected, even bewildering. He replies: "The hour has come for the Son of man to be glorified. Truly, truly, I say to you, unless a grain of wheat falls into the earth and dies, it remains alone; but if it dies, it bears much fruit" (John 12:23–24).

Wait a minute. The Apostles tell Jesus that some Greeks are here to see him, and he responds by saying his hour has come, and by speaking of death and fruit and grains of wheat? This surely must make sense—but how? The Apostles must have been baffled. They had made a simple request, and, in response, Jesus preached a sermon. We never even find out whether Jesus met with the Greeks!

There's a lot going on in this rich passage. Let's examine the details, one by one.

A LAMB IS BREAD FOR THIS

First, you'll notice that the exchange took place at Passover. The central rite of the Passover feast was the sacrifice of a spotless lamb. In John's Gospel, Jesus is explicitly called the "Lamb of God" (John 1:29, 36). The "hour" of the Lamb, then, is Passover. This particular Passover is more significant because, now, not just the children of Israel but the nations—the Gentiles, the Greeks—have come to find liberation.

So now would be a good time for Jesus to use the "lamb" metaphor, right? But he doesn't. He speaks of wheat instead, and he speaks of wheat "dying" to produce "much fruit." And how would that fruit manifest itself, once the grains were harvested? As bread, of course.

Now is *the hour*, Jesus says. It is Passover. Jesus is

the Lamb. And He is speaking of his own sacrifice. It becomes even more explicit in later verses, when, speaking again of his hour, he says, "Now is my soul troubled. And what shall I say? 'Father, save me from this *hour*?' No, for this purpose I have come to this *hour*. Father, glorify your name" (John 12:27–28).

We must not miss the importance of this moment in the divine drama. Jesus is offering himself here as the perfect sacrifice. We must be clear about this: he was offering *himself*. Jesus was not the hapless victim of a Roman execution; he was a victim of love. His life was not taken; it was given. (See also John 10:17–18.) Before Pilate, Caiaphas, or Herod could decree his death, Jesus gave up his life. Before anyone could lay a hand on him, he celebrated the Passover and he transformed the Passover into the Lord's Supper—the fruit of the grain of wheat, after it has fallen into the ground and died.

All this was, John tells us, "before the feast of the Passover, when Jesus knew that *his hour* had come to depart out of this world to the Father" (John 13:1). Just a few days later, we know from the other three Gospels, Jesus blessed the bread and the chalice of wine, pronouncing them to be his body and blood. Curiously, John's is the only Gospel that does not recount those particular details of the Passover meal. Yet John does tell us more about the rest of that supper. Toward the end of the meal, John relates, Jesus "lifted up his eyes to heaven and said, 'Father, *the hour* has come; glorify thy Son that the Son may glorify thee, since thou have given him power over all flesh, to give eternal life to all whom thou hast given him'" (John 17:1–2).

We know when this will happen: the hour. We know what will happen: human beings will participate in the glory and communion shared by the Father and the Son—"in the Spirit." In the passage, then, that interpreters call Jesus' "high-priestly prayer," the Lord prays: "that they may all be one; even as you, Father, are in me, and I in you, that they also may be [one] in us" (17:21). Don't miss the significance of what Jesus' hour will bring. Jesus is not saying that our oneness will be *like* the oneness of the Trinity; he's saying that our oneness will *be* the oneness of the Trinity. It will be not something similar but identical! In that hour, we will know the most intimate communion with God.

And, immediately after uttering this prayer, Jesus was arrested and carried off to be executed. With this event began the most literal, historical meaning of "the hour."

THE HOUR IS COMING

Besides the obvious literal meaning—the historic event of the cross—what else have we learned about Jesus' understanding of the hour? In the hour

- We receive wine, the best wine (John 2:1–11).
- We are empowered to worship in a new way—in spirit and truth (John 4:23–24).
- We hear God's Word in order to receive new life (John 5:25).
- We gather together as Gentiles and "Jews" to celebrate the new Passover (John 4:23, 12:20, 13:1).
- We receive the living bread, the fruit born of the grain of wheat that has died (John 12:24).
- We will see the Lamb of God lifted up, drawing all men to himself (John 12:32).

Take a second look at that list: bread and wine, the Word of the Lord, spiritual worship, a new Passover for Jews and Greeks. What does this add up to?

I was doing the math, even as I presented these findings to the students at Grove City so many years ago. Even the members of the college group began to see the sense in the questions I was asking.

Now, thirty-five years later, as I write these words, all but one of the members of that group are Catholic, and so am I. But I'm getting ahead of the story.

CHAPTER 11

The Chalices and the Church

By this time I had gained the habit of consulting the early Church Fathers for their biblical interpretations. My efforts were rewarded again and again.

They took the Bible seriously, and they often took it literally where we modern interpreters strain to find figurative readings. They read the Scriptures as a canonical whole, a coherent unity of Old Testament and New, and I found this deeply attractive. There was consistency and continuity in their approach to God's covenant. They saw no rupture or contradiction between the biblical covenants. And they ordered their churches in ways that surprised me—but ways that were profoundly faithful to the Scriptures.

Knowing what I knew about Jesus' Last Supper, I should not have been as surprised as I was when I discovered the value the early Church placed upon their cups—their chalices and other ritual vessels. Saint John

Chrysostom referred to the cup used in the Lord's Supper as "that dread cup, full of much power, and more precious than any created thing."[1]

Saint Ambrose of Milan said that the vessels used in the Lord's Supper could not, afterward, be used for any other purpose. No one was permitted to take them from the Church. If they were replaced or retired from use, they had to be destroyed—"broken up and afterwards melted down"—because they were considered sacred, "consecrated to . . . holy uses."[2] In his city the vessels were typically made of gold.[3] Nor was this unusual; the court records of the fourth-century North African martyrs—set down by a pagan stenographer—show that the Roman officials confiscated "two gold chalices" among the possessions of the Church.[4]

Tertullian, in the late 100s, describes liturgical chalices decorated with images of the Good Shepherd,[5] and such gilded cups have been found in excavations in the Roman catacombs.

The Church observed a profound reverence for the cups used in the Lord's Supper. When the enemies of Saint Athanasius wanted to seize him on trumped-up charges, they trumped up the most damaging crimes imaginable. They accused him of murder—and of intentionally breaking a chalice. The latter was considered the more serious crime.[6]

As an evangelical pastor, I found the Fathers' reverence startling. It went far beyond custodial care for the congregation's property. Where did it come from?

Well, the Fathers themselves did not hesitate to say. I learned the answer from the greatest Scripture scholar in the ancient Church, Saint Jerome of Stridon—a man who translated much of the Bible not just once but twice. In a letter to the Patriarch of Alexandria, he wrote:

> I admire in your work its practical aim, designed as it is to instruct by the authority of Scripture ignorant persons in all the churches concerning the reverence with which they must handle holy things and minister at Christ's altar; and to impress upon them that the sacred chalices, veils, and other accessories used in the celebration of the Lord's passion are not mere lifeless and senseless objects devoid of holiness, but that rather, from their association with the body and blood of the Lord, they are to be venerated with the same awe as the body and the blood themselves.[7]

I wondered whether I should count myself among those "ignorant persons" he mentions, because I did not handle such things as "holy." Nor did I believe that they had "real" contact with Jesus' body and blood. Bread and wine, in our rites, were just symbols. Although I was prepared to affirm that they were our most important symbols, I wasn't prepared to venerate them with awe, as Jerome thought I should.

But was I right in this? Or was Jerome? As I read the Fathers, and as I came to respect them as biblical interpreters, I was less sure of myself. If I were to find myself suddenly in a room with them, discussing the nature of Jesus' presence in the Eucharist—and the resulting reverence I owed to the cup—I would definitely stand alone in my evangelical doctrine of the sacrament.

Here is what I was discovering. The *Didache,* set down perhaps no later than A.D. 48, restricted communion only to believers and those who were free of serious sin.[8] Ignatius of Antioch, writing around A.D. 107, spoke of the elements of the Lord's Supper as "the flesh of our Savior"[9] and "the blood of God."[10] He said, in fact, that it was the very mark of infidelity and heresy to believe otherwise.[11]

Just a few years later we find Saint Justin Martyr using the same "realist" language to speak of the Lord's Supper. In his First Apology, addressed to the pagan Emperor Antoninus Pius, he explains: "the food which is blessed by the prayer of his word, and from which our blood and flesh by transmutation are nourished, is the flesh and blood of that Jesus who was made flesh."[12] He goes on to explain how this is so, drawing from the Gospel account of the Last Supper.

In the earliest Fathers I found another shocker. They had no scruple about calling the Lord's Supper a sacrifice. For Ignatius, the Church is "the altar" or "the place of sacrifice."[13] For Justin, the Eucharist is the sacrifice that definitively fulfills the Old Testament prophecy of Malachi:

> For from the rising of the sun to its setting my name is great among the nations, and in every place incense is offered to my name, and a pure offering; for my name is great among the nations, says the LORD of hosts. (Malachi 1:11)

Justin comments: "He then speaks of those Gentiles, namely us, who in every place offer sacrifices to him, i.e., the bread of the Eucharist, and also the cup of the Eucharist."[14]

The Eucharist as sacrifice ... the Eucharist as Real Presence ... I found these doctrines consistent among the Fathers and I found them to be continuous with the Scriptures—as the Fathers themselves insisted. I found the doctrines in the earliest Fathers (Tertullian, Irenaeus, Origen, Hippolytus) and then stated more precisely in the later Fathers (Cyril, Ambrose, Augustine, Chrysostom). The Fathers who were deepest in their knowledge of Scripture were most insistently realist in their approach to the sacrament. They had ready, deeply biblical reasons to speak of a "dread cup, full of much power."

Jerome and Chrysostom had learned their awe for the cup by reading the Scriptures. The Lord instructed Moses to have such vessels fashioned from gold (Exodus 25:29), and the people complied (Exodus 37:16). Joshua pronounced such vessels to be "sacred to the LORD" (Joshua 6:19). To King David these were the "holy vessels," and Ezra the Scribe agreed, as he said: "the vessels are holy" (Ezra 8:28). The Prophet Isaiah warned that anyone who bore "the vessels of the LORD" should be morally and ritually pure (Isaiah 52:11). And the Book of the Prophet Daniel (chapter 5) shows what happens when sacred vessels are not treated in a worthy manner.

I could find no reason to believe that reverence should be downgraded in the dispensation of the New Covenant. Jesus took a cup, blessed it, pronounced it to be the blood of the covenant. He identified the cup, moreover, with his redemptive suffering. And he commanded his disciples to take up a cup, in their turn, and "do this" as he had done.

Again, it seemed to me that this should call for *more* reverence, not less. If God was present in the Jerusalem Temple—in the glory cloud (see Ezekiel 10:3–4) and in the Bread of the Presence—how much more *real* should his presence be in the liturgy of the New Covenant?

MARTYR, HE WROTE

The Fathers showed not a shadow of doubt about the power of the Eucharistic cup. It was, they said, the source of their strength and courage. It was the reason they were able to do as Jesus did—not only in celebrating the Lord's Supper but also in dying as he did. Through the centuries of Roman persecution, the Fathers consistently spoke of martyrdom as a "cup."

The cup of martyrdom, in fact, was seen as the same cup that Jesus offered. Saint Polycarp of Smyrna, a disciple of the Apostle John, thanked God that he "should have a part in the number of your martyrs, in the cup of your Christ." His secretary, an eyewitness, tells us that Polycarp was bound to the stake like a sacrificial ram. In Polycarp's martyrdom we see the unmistakably significant convergence of Paschal symbols: the cup, the hour, and the animal victim.[15]

In the middle of the following century—at a time of intense persecution—Saint Cyprian of Carthage frequently used the "cup" as a synonym for martyrdom. Those who confess Jesus Christ "willingly drink the cup of martyrdom," he wrote.[16] It is by the cup of communion, he said elsewhere, that Christians are made "fit for the cup of martyrdom."[17] They were, in fact, seeking such strength *daily* from the Church. Cyprian explained:

A severer and a fiercer fight is now threatening, for which the soldiers of Christ ought to prepare themselves with uncorrupted faith and robust courage, considering that they drink the cup of Christ's blood daily, for the reason that they themselves also may be able to shed their blood for Christ.[18]

I had been viewed as eccentric when I increased the frequency of the Lord's Supper from quarterly to weekly. And here the early Fathers were testifying to daily communion—during times of extreme peril, when assembling as a congregation made Christians vulnerable to their persecutors.

I read on in the Fathers, and I learned that Tertullian considered the cup of Christian martyrdom to be a fulfillment of Revelation 17:6, where the allegorical figure Babylon grows drunk with the blood of the saints.[19] The cup that is the martyrs' blessing is a curse upon Babylon.

All of the Fathers' testimony seemed to track the Scriptures closely. Jesus repeatedly spoke of his own death as his "cup." When James and John asked him for the privilege of becoming his prime ministers, he asked them in turn: Are you able to drink the cup that I drink, or to be baptized with the baptism with which I am baptized? When they answered that they could, he said to them that they would indeed drink his cup and undergo his baptism (Mark 10:38), presumably meaning that they would share his suffering. It is significant that he described his suffering twice in sacramental terms—as a "baptism" and as a "cup."

In the upper room at the Last Supper, Jesus declared the third cup to contain his blood. A few hours later, in the Garden of Gethsemane, he begged in prayer that the cup of suffering might pass from him (Mark 14:36). And then, when Peter rose to defend him from his would-be executioners, Jesus said to Peter, "Put your sword into its sheath; shall I not drink the cup which the Father has given me?" (John 18:11).

The cup was martyrdom, for Jesus as for Cyprian—and many thousands of other Christians in the Roman Empire. Yet they willingly took it up. Saint Augustine made the connection clear: "But what is to receive the cup of salvation, but to imitate the Passion of our Lord? . . . I will receive the cup of Christ, I will drink of our Lord's Passion."[20]

Jesus wanted the sacraments to be an imitation of his life and a communion with his life. They were symbols, as I had been taught, but not just symbols. They were symbols invested with divine power. There was awesome power, fearsome power, "dread power," in the cup of the Lord's Passion.

FAITH UP TO THE FAQS

There comes a moment when a critic must turn his criticism upon himself. For me that moment had come. When people remarked that my beliefs seemed Catholic to them, I insisted that they could not be. Why? Well, because I knew, for example, that Catholics believed that Jesus was repeatedly sacrificed in the Mass, and that clearly contradicted Scripture.

But how did I know that Catholics believed such things?

I had read it in books written by authors I trusted.

Yet now I was reading the works of the martyrs of the early Church, and I was learning to trust them in matters of Scriptural interpretation. And I saw that they believed the Eucharist to be a "sacrifice" of real flesh and blood. Nevertheless, they spoke nowhere about killing Jesus again, or sacrificing him repeatedly.

I decided to check a Catholic account of Catholic beliefs. At the time (the early 1980s), there was no more commonly cited Catholic authority than the Baltimore Catechism. It was a simple, question-and-answer compendium of basic doctrines. And it taught clearly that the Mass was not a repeated sacrifice.[21] It was, rather, the same sacrifice as the cross. The catechism went on to address the matter in some detail, though still in simple terms:

Q. Is the Mass the same sacrifice as that of the Cross?

A. The Mass is the same sacrifice as that of the Cross.

Q. How is the Mass the same sacrifice as that of the Cross?

A. The Mass is the same sacrifice as that of the Cross because the offering and the priest are the same—Christ our Blessed Lord; and the ends for which the sacrifice of the Mass is offered are the same as those of the sacrifice of the Cross . . .

Q. Is there any difference between the sacrifice of the Cross and the sacrifice of the Mass?

A. Yes; the manner in which the sacrifice is offered is different. On the Cross Christ really shed His blood and was really slain; in the Mass there is no real shedding of blood nor real death, because Christ can die no more; but the sacrifice of the Mass, through the separate consecration of the bread and the wine, represents His death on the Cross.[22]

This was all news to me—yet it was drawn from the basic textbook of Catholic faith, used by millions of grade school students through the first half of the twentieth century. It seemed to directly contradict what I had learned from non-Catholic, anti-Catholic sources.

What's more, the passage served as a kind of theological summary and synthesis of what I had found in the early Church Fathers. What was implicit in the Fathers' exhortations was explicit in these numbered questions and answers.

This did not make me a Catholic. But it did make me self-critical, and I was ready to repent of my false prejudices and the bigotry I had so casually accepted.

It also opened new avenues—boulevards, really—in my reading and research. I discovered a world of profound scholarship I had formerly only glimpsed in footnotes. Soon I was taking classes at a Catholic university and discovering one or two others who shared my fascination with the biblical covenants. And then I was applying to a Catholic institution, Marquette University in Milwaukee, for doctoral studies.

I was not yet ready to take up the cup with Catholics. But I was more than ready to read the Bible with them.

CHAPTER 12

The Paschal Shape
of the Liturgy

I had still, in fact, never attended a Catholic Mass. I no longer felt revulsion or horror at the mention of Catholic rites and customs and theology. I now found myself reading many Catholic authors—and feeling less shame for it the more I read.

Going to Mass, though, seemed like a giant step. I knew from reading the Fathers that the Eucharistic liturgy was a covenant ritual, an occasion of utmost solemnity. It wasn't like going to a movie, or going to the symphony, or even going to a Sunday service at an evangelical church. If the Catholics were right about the meaning of the Mass, mere attendance was a potentially seismic event in the spiritual order. Was I ready for that? If the Catholics were wrong, of course, then their Mass was the greatest blasphemy possible—and I wanted no part of that. In thinking about the Mass, there was no safe middle ground.

The more I read the work of Catholic scholars, the more I thought it impossible that the Mass could be blasphemy. I knew from Scripture that "no one can say 'Jesus is Lord' except by the Holy Spirit" (1 Corinthians 12:3). I knew also that "if you confess with your lips that Jesus is Lord and believe in your heart that God raised him from the dead, you will be saved" (Romans 10:9). The authors of the books were men thoroughly convinced of Jesus' true divinity, true humanity, and bodily resurrection. They were eager to proclaim Jesus as risen Lord. They could do so "only by the Holy Spirit," and no one who practiced blasphemous worship could be living in the Spirit.

So one day, well into my first semester as a doctoral student at Marquette, I mustered the courage to go. I would be no more than an observer—an academic making a historical investigation. I decided to go to one of the weekday Masses, since I knew they drew smaller crowds than Sunday Mass. With my Bible and a notebook, I took a seat in the back pew at the university chapel. I was well prepared. I had taken every precaution. I could not have been safer if I'd been locked in a plastic observation bubble.

But I soon found out that I wasn't prepared at all. What I was experiencing was an immersion in Scripture—both the Old Testament and the New. But it wasn't at all like a Bible study. It wasn't at all like a class. There was nothing about it that anyone would find entertaining. There was nothing that seemed calculated or calibrated to stir my emotions.

The words and the worship were directed to God. They were about God. The ritual forms were deeply Trinitarian, like the blessings and greetings of Saint Paul. When people weren't reading directly from the Bible, the priest was pronouncing prayers rich with Scriptural quotations and allusions that ranged freely from Genesis to Revelation.

But especially Revelation. Almost everything I saw at the chapel reminded me of that last book in the canon. There was an altar and vested clergy. There were golden lampstands. People sang the song of the angels in heaven: "Holy, Holy, Holy." And, again and again, there was mention of Jesus as "the Lamb."

The rite of the Mass was evoking heaven—as if we were really there—and there was a Paschal quality to the entire event. It wasn't just in the mention of "the Lamb," though indeed that makes sense only in reference to the Passover of Jesus. The entire Mass was rich with Paschal symbols. I noticed many of them that first day, and more still as I returned to Mass in the days that followed.

I could not help but conclude that the covenant

renewal celebrated by Catholics was consistent and continuous (as a fulfillment) with the covenant renewal celebrated by ancient Israel. It was also profoundly Scriptural and Christ-centered.

Let's consider the most obviously Paschal parts of the Mass, those that would be recognized by anyone familiar with the seder.

HEARD OF LAMBS

The Lamb is the most obvious Paschal reference in the Mass. Although the prayers mention other Old Testament rites—e.g., the meal of Melchizidek (Genesis 14:18–20)—the Lamb dominates.

It is mentioned, early in the Mass, in the Gloria: "Lord God, Lamb of God, Son of the Father, you take away the sins of the world."

The Lamb is mentioned five times in a short space during the Communion Rite:

> ALL: *Lamb* of God, you take away the sins of the world: have mercy on us. *Lamb* of God, you take away the sins of the world: have mercy on us. *Lamb* of God, you take away the sins of the world: grant us peace.

PRIEST: Behold the *Lamb* of God, who takes away the sin of the world. Blessed are those called to the supper of the *Lamb*.

In one of the popular Eucharistic prayers, too, Jesus is invoked as Lamb, though the word itself does not appear. The First Eucharistic Prayer for Reconciliation begins the institution narrative by establishing an explicit context of Passover and covenant renewal: "But before his arms were outstretched between heaven and earth, to become the lasting sign of your covenant, he desired to celebrate the Passover with his disciples." The prayer then goes on to describe the Mass itself in Paschal terms as "the memorial of your Son Jesus Christ, who is our Passover and our surest peace." Like Saint Paul (1 Corinthians 5:7), the prayer uses "Passover" as an abbreviated equivalent of "Passover lamb."

As at the Passover, so at the Mass: the prayers establish the character of the event. It is a solemn "banquet of the Lamb." It is a sacrifice, and the victim is "the Lamb." The blood of the Lamb brings "mercy" to God's Chosen People.

HALLEL CAN YOU GO

Another characteristically Paschal prayer is the "Alleluia," sung or recited before the Gospel. It's just a single word, and it's so commonly used that we hardly notice it. But it is significant here because the Jews of Jesus' time associated the word primarily with the Passover.

The early Church so valued the word that it was left untranslated in biblical and liturgical texts (see Revelation 19:1–6). Like the Hebrew "Amen," it was considered sacred for what it expressed. "Alleluia" (or "Hallelujah") means, literally, "Praise the Lord!" It represents the dominant theme of a group of the Psalms that are distinctive for the effusive honor they give to the Almighty for his deeds of creation and redemption. As I mentioned earlier, these are collectively called the Hallel, which is Hebrew for "praise."

On Passover, these festive biblical hymns were sung at table during the seder meal. The ritual divided them into two groupings, one long (the Great Hallel) and the other relatively short (the Little Hallel).

According to the Mishnah, there was, in the first century, a dispute over which Psalms should constitute these groupings.[1] The school of the rabbi Shammai prescribed Psalm 113 alone as the Little Hallel, but the school of the rabbi Hillel paired 113 with 114. We do not know which grouping was favored by Jesus and his disciples.

In any event, the Little Hallel was sung before the dinner began. The Great Hallel, the long sequence of Psalms 115 through 118, was sung with the fourth cup.[2] This is the "hymn" that Jesus and the eleven sang as they left the upper room and walked to the Garden of Gethsemane.

The Catholic Church, in its meal of covenant renewal, sometimes employs one or another of the Hallel Psalms as a reading. But it preserves the spirit of these Passover songs in the Alleluia recited or sung before the Gospel.

In Lent, the Church suppresses the Alleluia. Why? Because Lent is a season of preparation for the Christian Passover: Easter. When Catholics (in the West especially) turn the calendar page from Lent to Easter, the word "Alleluia" does not merely return to its normal place before the Gospel; rather, it saturates the prayers of the Mass for the entire fifty-day Easter Season. For Christians, as for the Jews of Jesus' time—and Jesus himself—"Alleluia" is the term most characteristic of the Passover. In the words beloved by Pope Saint John Paul II: "We are an Easter people, and [therefore] alleluia is our song."[3]

AN OFFERING YOU CAN'T REFUSE

A pivotal point in the Mass—where the liturgy turns from the readings to the offering—is the offertory. It is then, perhaps, that the prayers are most recognizably Paschal.

Consider first these blessings from the Passover seder. The first is pronounced over unleavened bread, and the second over a cup of wine. If you're a Catholic—or even if you're a non-Catholic who's attended Mass—the words should have a familiar ring about them.

> Blessed are You, Lord, our God, King of the Universe, who creates the fruit of the earth. Amen.
>
> Blessed are You, Lord, our God, King of the Universe, creator of the fruit of the vine. Amen.

And here are the blessings pronounced with the bread and wine at the offertory of the Mass.

> Blessed are you, Lord God of all creation, for through your goodness we have received the bread we offer you: fruit of the earth and work of human hands, it will become for us the bread of life.

> Blessed are you, Lord God of all creation, for
> through your goodness we have received the
> wine we offer you: fruit of the vine and work of
> human hands, it will become our spiritual drink.

You don't need an advanced degree in history or Hebrew to see the development here. The traditional table
blessings used at the seder have been supplemented to
note the Passover's fulfillment in Jesus Christ—and,
specifically, Jesus Christ as he is about to appear, really
present, in the Eucharist.

Even I, as I sat in the chapel at Marquette—a life-
long Protestant coming in cold—recognized the origin
of these prayers and saw what the Church was doing
with them.

INTO THE MIX

I recognized Passover not only in the words of the offertory but also in the actions. I hardly need mention
the obvious: the basic elements that were offered were
unleavened bread and wine. Wine would have been customary at any Jewish banquet, as would bread; but *unleavened* bread was peculiar to one feast: Passover.

Even the way the priest prepared the wine was red-
olent of the Jewish feast. The Jews, like most ancient

peoples, drank their wine mixed.[4] They stored the "fruit of the vine" in a strong, concentrated form and then diluted it before serving it in cups. I knew of this custom not only from the seder but also from the Old Testament, which speaks in such terms of the mixed cups at banquets: "wine, well mixed" (Psalm 75:8; see also Proverbs 9:2). The Mishnah's account of the seder makes many references to this: "When they have mixed the first cup. . . . They mixed for him a second cup of wine. . . . They mixed the third cup for him."[5]

As I've noted, even the poor were guaranteed their four cups at the seder, and the Talmud prescribed proportions for the mixture, so that no one should have to celebrate with wine that was lacking in flavor and potency.

The early Church continued the practice. The account we find in Justin Martyr's First Apology provides an elegant witness. Set down around A.D. 150, it suggests the words and actions of the Passover seder—and the Mass as celebrated the day I walked into the chapel. "There is then brought to the president of the brethren bread and a cup of wine mixed with water; and he, taking them, gives praise and glory to the Father of the universe."[6]

Later in the same century, the practice of the mixed cup at Mass is confirmed twice by Saint Irenaeus. He notes in one place: "When, therefore, the mingled cup and the manufactured bread receives the Word of God, ... the Eucharist of the blood and the body of Christ is made."[7] In another place he affirms, citing Jesus' authority, that "the mixture in the cup is his blood."[8]

Saint Cyprian said there were many good reasons for mixing wine and water in the Mass. The most important, though, was the example of Jesus.[9] Cyprian also ventured allegorical interpretations of the mingling of water and wine, saying that the wine represented Jesus and the water the Church on earth.[10] (Irenaeus agreed with him on that point.) Saint Ambrose held that the wine and water vividly suggested the blood and water that flowed from Jesus' side as he hung on the cross (John 19:34).[11]

MARQUETTE VALUE

As becomes apparent, the Mass echoes the Passover liturgy in many ways, not only in small details but in its overall structure. It includes active remembrance in its prescribed readings (the Liturgy of the Word). It includes the consumption of a sacrifice (the Liturgy of the Eucharist). In the Passover, the sacrificial victim is the lamb. In the Mass, the victim is the Lamb of God, who took unleavened bread and declared it to be his body.

Saint Paul's exhortation, of course, bears repeating here: "For Christ, our paschal lamb, has been sacrificed. Let us, therefore, celebrate the festival, not with the old leaven, the leaven of malice and evil, but with the unleavened bread of sincerity and truth" (1 Corinthians 5:7–8).

At Marquette I was beginning to discover historians of liturgy who compared the structure of the Mass to the ancient Jewish liturgies and analyzed the parts as well as the whole. They noted that the most essential part of the Mass was its haggadah, the narrative of institution in the Eucharistic Prayer. There, using the words of Jesus, the priest pronounced the blessing and described the significance of the items before him on the table. Scholars from Louis Bouyer in France to Enrico Mazza in Italy noted that the typical Catholic Eucharistic prayer follows the structure and themes of the Jewish blessing over bread (*birkat ha-mazon*).

At some point I happened upon a book titled *The Eucharist in the Primitive Church*, by Edward J. Kilmartin, S.J., and in it I found a fascinating discussion of the influence of Passover traditions on the early Christian liturgy. But I found something else, and it stopped me short. Father Kilmartin ventured a definition that could apply to both the seder and the Mass. After stating his thesis, he broke it down as a list for further analysis. I'd like to present it here, slightly adapted.

It is a liturgical feast involving sacrifice . . .

. . . and an accompanying cultic banquet . . .

. . . celebrated by the community . . .

. . . of the chosen people . . .

. . . accomplished in the present, it commemorates a past deliverance

. . . and looks forward to a future definitive intervention of Yahweh.[12]

Intellectually, I grasped that as I sat and filled notebooks in Marquette's theological library. But the reality of it grasped me as I sat in the back pew of the university chapel day after day.

I quite literally hungered for the Eucharist, which I came to know was "Christ our Passover." The hunger was evident in an embarrassing way the first time I went to Mass. At the consecration I found myself salivating—and weeping—as I realized it was really Jesus, and he was offering his own flesh to me as "living bread come down from heaven."

CHAPTER 13

The Christian Passover

I wanted communion with Christ. I wanted to drink his cup, with his Church, even if that meant suffering and sacrifice would follow. My wife, Kimberly, opposed my becoming Catholic. A Presbyterian pastor's daughter whose brothers were pastors, she could not bring herself to understand what was happening to me—and to her life, the life we had carefully planned together. Some of our friends told her that divorce would be justifiable, but divorce was even more abominable to her than what she imagined Catholicism to be (what I had once imagined Catholicism to be).

At first I promised her that I would wait five years to enter the Church. But every day felt like five years, and I was sure I could not bear it more than a thousand times. I begged her to release me from my promise, and she did.

By this time I knew some of the local pastors, and I rushed to one and made my plea for admission without delay. It was already Lent. Monsignor Fabian Bruskewitz considered the situation. I was a doctoral student in theology. I held a master's degree in theology. I had intensively studied the Scriptures, the Fathers, and the tradition. He concluded that I knew enough to make an informed decision and that I was ready.

At Easter Vigil, Monsignor Bruskewitz gave me the sacramental "grand slam" of conditional Baptism, Holy Communion, and Confirmation. And afterward I saw things differently. Now the hard sayings of Jesus—about baptismal regeneration, about his Real Presence, about sacramental absolution—began to make sense down deep in my soul, in my mind, and in my bones.

I could not know, during Lent of 1986, that Easter Vigil would bring a decisive turn in the road, not just for me but also for Kimberly. Though she grieved that night, and even called it the worst night of her life, she also began to notice just how profoundly biblical were the rites of the Catholic Church. If you count the Responsorial Psalms, there are seventeen long Scripture readings in the course of the liturgy. That's more Bible than she, a pastor's kid, had ever heard at a Sunday service.

In a few more years, she would undergo the rites herself.

DAYS OF FUTURE PASCH

Easter is today more important to me (and to Kimberly) than any other day on the calendar. It's more important than our birthdays and even our wedding anniversary. It marks the day that new life, the fullness of life, began for us. It is the day we received God's mercy in unimaginable abundance. It is the day he "passed over" our household because we were washed in the blood of the true Lamb.

Easter is Passover, and the early Christians celebrated it as such. In fact, they called the holiday "Passover," and most modern languages still use the same word to describe both the Jewish holiday we know as Passover and the Christian holiday we know as Easter. They use words taken from the Hebrew *Pesach*. Spaniards call it *Pascua*, Italians *Pasqua*. The Dutch say *Pasen*. In Zulu it's *IPhasika*. All these terms derive from *Pesach*. Only a few languages—English, German, Polish—call the feast by a word unrelated to Passover.

It was the first Christian holiday to be observed each year. We don't know when that custom began, but we see the first evidence of it very early in the second century—and the Fathers of that time insisted that their tradition went back to the Apostles. The Christian rite was not a seder but rather a reading of the story of Jesus' Passion and resurrection, interspersed with preaching and conferral of the sacraments of initiation: Baptism, Confirmation (Chrismation), and Eucharist. The vigil service began late in the evening and ended at sunrise on the day of the Resurrection. It was customary then, as it is today, to receive new converts into the Church during the Easter Vigil liturgy.

Scripture tells us that the early Church placed a premium on unity. "Now the company of those who believed were of one heart and soul" (Acts 4:32). Passover was the only matter so important that it could threaten that bond. What was the controversy?

Many Christians in the East kept the custom—which they attributed to the Apostle John—of observing the Resurrection on the *date* of Passover every year. Since Passover falls on the fourteenth day of the Hebrew month of Nisan, these Christians were called Quartodecimans, which literally means "Fourteeners."

In the West, however, the Church had always marked the feast on the Sunday after Passover (unless Passover fell on a Sunday), thus emphasizing the importance of the Lord's Day as the day of the Resurrection.

The popes in the West threatened the churches in the East with excommunication. Bishops (notably Polycarp and Irenaeus), in turn, made pleas for mutual tolerance. And both customs coexisted uneasily for centuries. But Passover mattered so much that the Church ultimately could not live with the strain. In 325 the Council of

Nicaea settled the matter definitively by imposing the Sunday observance of *Pascha* on the whole Church.

The evidence we have suggests that the early Church marked its feast as a comprehensive celebration of Jesus' suffering, death, and rising. These together constituted the Paschal Mystery.

Passover commemorated the sacrifice of Jesus once for all. But it also commemorated the application of the grace of Jesus' sacrifice to believers, year after year, generation after generation. Jesus said to his disciples: "The cup that I drink you will drink; and with the baptism with which I am baptized, you will be baptized" (Mark 10:39). And believers experience the Paschal Mystery in Baptism and in the Eucharist—the cup. We know Passover as a sacrifice, but also as a mystery—as sacraments. The bread we break is a real communion in the Lord's body; the cup we share is a true communion in his blood, which is the blood of the covenant. There is nothing more authentic, more genuine, than this. Catholics use terms like "Real Presence" for good reason. Like Saint Paul, we celebrate the feast with the unleavened bread of sincerity and truth—and that bread is truly the flesh, the body, of Jesus, the Lamb of God.

NO PAIN, NO REIGN

My friends who had known me at Gordon-Conwell Seminary were shocked to hear of my conversion. They called, and they were more shocked to hear me talk this way. I strove to move our conversations away from Catholic-Protestant differences, so that we could begin on common ground.

Both Catholics and Protestants agree, I assured them, that Jesus' sacrifice took place on Calvary "once for all" (Hebrews 7:27 and 10:10; 1 Peter 3:18). There is no saving sacrifice apart from the cross.

But there was nothing on Calvary that would have suggested sacrifice to a first-century Jew. No devout Jews witnessing Jesus' crucifixion would have gone home and recounted what they witnessed in terms of a sacrifice. For them, a sacrifice had to take place inside the Temple, at an altar, with a Levitical priest presiding. Jesus' crucifixion took place outside the walls, where there was no Temple, no Levite, no altar. It looked like a bloody Roman execution, not a sacrifice.

What was it, then, that transformed Jesus' execution into a sacrifice?

The transformative moment was Jesus' offering of his body and blood at the Last Supper. Jesus spoke of that offering in sacrificial terms, commanding his Apostles to keep it in perpetuity as his memorial: "Do this in remembrance of me." He called it the New Covenant (Luke 22:20), echoing Moses' words as he ratified the Old Law with a sacrifice (Exodus 24:8). The Apostles, too, looked upon his memorial in sacrificial terms: "For Christ, our paschal lamb, has been sacrificed" (1 Corinthians 5:7). Even the elements on the table signified the sacrificial separation of flesh (bread) and blood (wine).

The Last Supper is what transformed Good Friday from an execution into a sacrifice—and Easter Sunday is what transformed the sacrifice into a sacrament. Christ's body was raised in glory, so it is now communicable to the faithful. Indeed, the Eucharist is the *same* sacrifice he offered by instituting the Eucharist and then dying on Calvary; only now his sacred humanity is deified and deifying. It is the high-priestly sacrifice that he offers in heaven and on earth.

That's the holy sacrifice of the Mass. If the Eucharist were only a meal, then Calvary would be no more than an execution.

It would be difficult to overestimate the importance of Jesus' Eucharistic action. The institution narrative appears in all three Synoptic Gospels as well as in Paul's Letter to the Corinthians. It represents Paul's most extensive quotation of Jesus' words. The theologian Robert Daly called the words of institution—"This is my body . . . my blood"—"a prophecy-in-act anticipation of Jesus' death, a revelation of Christ's saving action which pointed towards and explained the significance of Jesus' death."[1]

Jesus' priestly offering at the Last Supper transformed his crucifixion at Calvary from an execution into a sacrifice. The Paschal Mystery, moreover, brought the ancient observances to fulfillment. I found a succinct explanation in one of the standard ecumenical textbooks on worship.

> The Passover of Christ fulfilled and transcended the Jewish Passover. It is in the Passover context that the Eucharist was instituted, thus indicating that it is through the Eucharist that the Passover of Christ, his redeeming work, is made available to all. It is of the Passover of Christ that the Eucharist is the *anamnesis,* or memorial. Just as the paschal mystery was the culmination of Christ's redeeming work, so the Eucharist becomes the culmination and center of Christian worship.[2]

Some of my seminary classmates and former colleagues in ministry were willing to listen to me—at first because that's the only way they could speak to what they saw as the "error of my ways." But eventually some of them—and not just a few—were willing to join me at the Lord's Table for the cup of blessing.

HOW MUCH DOES PENTECOST?

I awoke elated on Easter Sunday in 1986, and I remained so for a long time. For Catholics, the Passover is not the matter of a day. The Paschal Octave lasts eight days, all of which are celebrated like Sundays. The Church sings the Gloria at every Mass. And the joy goes on still further. The Paschal Season extends till the great feast of Pentecost.

Pentecost is a supremely important feast, which I think is sorely neglected in our day. It is, in any event, profoundly related to the themes of this book—Passover and the fourth cup—and so it merits our attention.

Of all the feasts on the old Jewish calendar, only two have endured as Christian feasts: Passover and Pentecost. These two, with Sukkot, the "Feast of Booths," were the three pilgrimage festivals of ancient Judaism. The Book of Exodus (23:14–17) required all Israelite males to celebrate these three feasts in the holy city, Jerusalem.

Passover and Pentecost were inextricably bound to one another. Pentecost, in fact, gets its very name from its relation to Passover. *Pentecost* comes from the Greek word for "fiftieth"; Pentecost is the fiftieth day after Passover.

Jews in the first century commemorated the Exodus on Passover. On Pentecost they celebrated God's gift of the Law at Mount Sinai. The first event was ordered to the second. The Israelites were set free not so that they could wander aimlessly but so that they could walk in God's ways—the ways set out for them in the Ten Commandments. In the Old Covenant, Passover happened for the sake of Pentecost. Passover was arguably the more solemn commemoration—the highest point on the calendar—but it required the later feast for its completion.

We find the same dynamic at work in the New Covenant. Jesus' Passover points forward to fulfillment with the gift of the Spirit in the Christian Pentecost. In the fourth Gospel we see Jesus repeatedly making this point, and he does so at the Last Supper, his Passover meal! He tells his disciples that the Counselor, sent by the Father, would bring the work of Jesus to completion (John 14:16, 26; 15:26; 16:7).

Saints and scholars down through the centuries have been quick to notice another, more subtle correspondence.

When Jesus takes the Paschal fourth cup, he is suffering on the cross. It is given to him from a sponge attached to a hyssop branch (the same type of branch

Moses commanded to be used for sprinkling the blood of the covenant; see Exodus 12:22). Saint John, an eyewitness, chose his words carefully as he described what happened in that moment—and God inspired him in every word he chose.

"When Jesus had received the vinegar," John tells us, "he said, 'It is finished'; and he bowed his head and gave up his spirit" (John 19:30).

I cannot help, here, but recall the question: *What* is finished?

The Passover is finished. The Passover has been fulfilled. It began the evening before as the Passover of the Old Covenant, but it now finds fulfillment on the cross on Good Friday—as the Passover of the New Covenant.

Jesus has taken the fourth cup. Everything has been fulfilled. And, in that fulfillment, he "gave up his spirit," thus foreshadowing the gift that would come to the Church on Pentecost. It is worth noting that he also, according to John's account, "from that hour" (19:27) gave up his mother and his sacramental blood and water (19:34), all as gifts to the Church of his beloved disciples.

The sacrifice was done, once for all. The Passover had been transformed. Now all that remained was its application to the Church forever.

CHAPTER 14

The Paschal Shape of Life

What I have laid down in these pages is an account of my life—or at least a small portion of my life. It is certainly a larger account than I've given in any of my previous talks or essays on "The Fourth Cup." I've done it because I felt called to do it.

But even a big book would be a relatively small calling within Jesus' larger call to you and me. Our vocation is to lay down not merely the stories of our lives but the whole of our lives. That is our common vocation. It is the cup we've taken up, the baptism with which we've been baptized.

Jesus said:

> For this reason the Father loves me, because I lay down my life, that I may take it again. No one takes it from me, but I lay it down of my own accord. I have power to lay it down, and I

have power to take it again; this charge I have received from my Father. (John 10:17–18)

We lay down our lives by taking up his cross. Note that he spoke not just to a select, small group but to "the multitude," when he said: "If any man would come after me, let him deny himself and take up his cross and follow me" (Mark 8:34).

This is the message of the Last Supper. This is the paradox that Christians call the Paschal Mystery: "whoever loses his life for my sake and the gospel's will save it" (Mark 8:35). At that seder meal, Jesus declared the unleavened bread to be his body and the blessing cup to hold his blood. This was not a metaphor. It was what philosophers call a "speech-act," comparable to the word by which God created the world (see Hebrews 11:3). "For he spoke, and it came to be; he commanded, and it stood forth" (Psalm 33:9). This has been the constant faith of Christians since the first generation. It has been their lifeblood—*our* lifeblood.

The Paschal Mystery was not simply a series of historic events that took place around A.D. 30. The Paschal Mystery was something that the early Christians *entered* and shared—something they took up, as a cup—every Sunday when they attended the Eucharist.

Taking up the cup voluntarily, they accepted the invitation of Jesus to drink the cup of pain that he drank (Mark 10:38–39). The early Christians laid down their lives voluntarily—even to the point of martyrdom—just like Isaac, who went willingly to be his father's sacrifice, and just like every other "sacrificial lamb" since the foundation of the world. The martyrs could not have done this on their own. They received their strength from the cup of Christ, which renewed the covenant and bestowed the life of grace.

What Jesus accomplished, and what he made possible, was the perfect self-offering of an unblemished victim with a willing disposition. Only he could do this, because only he possessed the sinless perfection of God.

Nevertheless, he is not alone, because he willed to share that power. He willed to share the redemptive power of his suffering with anyone who accepted his invitation to drink the cup that held his blood. This is the power that enabled Saint Paul to proclaim: "Now I rejoice in my sufferings for your sake, and in my flesh I complete what is lacking in Christ's afflictions for the sake of his body, that is, the Church" (Colossians 1:24). He could rejoice in his sufferings, because he knew that his sufferings were redemptive, united as they were in a holy communion with the suffering of Jesus.

In a sense, there is nothing new about any of these principles. They were hidden in plain sight since the foundation of the world. In another sense, Jesus' self-offering is utterly new, because it is now achieved, revealed, and communicated.

CUP OF SORROW

The Church Fathers saw the connection. Saint Augustine asked: "But what is to receive the cup of salvation, but to imitate the Passion of our Lord? . . . I will receive the cup of Christ, I will drink of our Lord's Passion."[1] For the holy bishop of Hippo, the cup is a grace offered to free human beings, who must will to receive and drink it.

It is a profound mystery why anyone would reject such an offer from Jesus Christ. It's not as if, by doing so, they can avoid suffering altogether. Suffering, Augustine explained, has been our lot since Adam mixed "our cup of sorrow . . . our cup of toil." "From this *cup of sorrow* no one may be excused" (emphasis added). Every baby's cry, he said, bears witness to this.[2]

Suffering is inevitable, as inexorable as death. Yet our nature resists it. We seek reflexively to avoid pain at any cost—even, sometimes, at the cost of our future.

We see the dynamic at work even in Jesus, the perfect man. From his Passover seder he proceeded to the Garden of Gethsemane, where he endured a violent agony. He fell on his face and prayed, "My Father, if it be possible, let this cup pass from me" (Matthew 26:39). His sweat fell with drops of blood to the ground. This is the furthest limit of human sorrow. Jesus, as God, possesses full knowledge of the tortures to come. His body responds with extreme revulsion and resistance. That's only natural. But he responds with acceptance, submission: "nevertheless not my will, but yours, be done" (Luke 22:42).

The drama of Jesus and the cup is supremely important. It's essential that we get it right. Jesus is not a fearless man. He is not some freakish superhero, so different from us that we cannot learn from him. Jesus experiences a genuine physical fear. But his fears are rightly ordered. Yes, he resists the cup of sorrow, the cup of toil. Yes, he fears what is to come. But these are not his greatest fears. Still greater is his aversion to *anything other than his Father's will.*

Fear is only natural. God created it and instilled it in us as a salutary instinct. Thus, fear is good. It leads us to preserve our bodily life.

But Jesus shows us that there are greater things than bodily life. There is divine life, which he will share with us—if we live as he lived and die as he died. We call this life "heaven," but it is not something distant in space and time. It began in us with our Baptism, and it grows in us every time we take up the Eucharistic cup.

God wants us to live with him forever. In his mercy, however, he acclimates us to that life right now. He holds it out to us in the blessing cup.

KNOW PAIN, NO GAIN

This life would otherwise be impossible for us to live. By nature we lack the capacity to live as God lives and love as God loves. If we want to experience the love, joy, and peace of heaven right now, then we need to experience it in Jesus, the God-Man.

This does not mean we will be exempt from suffering. We must be emphatic about this point. Saint Paul was a greater saint than you and I will ever be, but he didn't get a free pass. Remember, he said that he *rejoiced* in his sufferings—and he wasn't talking about hangnails or the common cold.

> Three times I have been beaten with rods; once I was stoned. Three times I have been shipwrecked; a night and a day I have been adrift at sea; on frequent journeys, in danger from rivers, danger from robbers, danger from my own people, danger from Gentiles, danger in the city, danger in the wilderness, danger at sea, danger from false brethren; in toil and hard-

ship, through many a sleepless night, in hunger and thirst, often without food, in cold and exposure. And, apart from other things, there is the daily pressure upon me of my anxiety for all the churches. Who is weak, and I am not weak? (2 Corinthians 11:25–29)

Indeed, Paul talks about his sufferings as a crucifixion, which he gladly accepts.

I have been crucified with Christ; it is no longer I who live, but Christ who lives in me; and the life I now live in the flesh I live by faith in the Son of God, who loved me and gave himself for me. (Galatians 2:20)

If Jesus and Paul were not exempt from suffering, neither should we expect to be.

Think of the Israelites at the hour of the first Passover. With great miracles, God delivered them from slavery. Yet they forgot their divine savior as soon as they felt the first weariness of wandering, the first twinge of hunger, the first sensation of thirst. They abandoned God and turned to idols.

The Jewish philosopher Philo of Alexandria observed that the Israelites had missed the very point of the Passover. God established the symbols of the seder to lead his people to live virtuous lives, with their fears and desires rightly ordered—and everything subordinated to the divine will. From the bread of the Passover the Hebrews should have learned to reject the leaven of pride. From the bitter herbs they should have learned a certain indifference to ease and sweetness. From the lamb hastily roasted they should have learned to do without seasonings and luxury. From the seder they were supposed to learn to discipline their bodies and wills.[3]

The Chosen People failed, but their failure was providential, so that the whole human race might come to know its own helplessness to avoid sin, its inability to do lasting good.

The power over sin—the power to do good—would come only with the baptism and blessing cup of Jesus.

PASS OVER THE PUNS

In their preaching, the Fathers delighted in punning on the word "Passover." In Greek, as in English, the word (*Pascha*) resembles the term for "passion" or suffering (*pascho*).

The Fathers weren't being masochistic or morbid. They were simply recognizing the conditions of life on earth. It is significant that the oldest extended meditation on the Passion of Christ focuses not on his physical pain but on his moral suffering in the Garden. Saint Maximus Confessor chose to preach not on the nails tearing the flesh but on Jesus' inner struggle to accept the fourth cup.

Jesus' love for us is expressed perfectly in his hour, his cup, his suffering—in the Paschal Mystery. We are prone to forget this. We want to experience love as pleasure. We want to imagine love that way. And it's true indeed that there is no higher pleasure than love.

Yet love as the occasion of those pleasing sensations— the enjoyment of someone else's presence—is not identical with those pleasing sensations. And love can thrive in the absence of pleasure. Think of a wife caring for a husband with advanced dementia. She no longer knows the delight of his conversation. He no longer buys her gifts or sends her flowers. His body, once handsome, is now heavy as she lifts him from his chair and guides him to the table.

She is suffering for the sake of another. She is giving selflessly, as Christ gave. She knows the hard joy that is true love.

I know of a man in similar circumstances, very old and caring full-time for his ailing wife. His oldest son worried aloud, one day, that caregiving was going to kill his dad. The dad just raised an eyebrow and responded: "You'd rather I die on the golf course?"

Where would the father have died more happily,

enjoying himself on the putting green or *giving himself* in love at home?

Pope Benedict XVI spoke truth in an impromptu interview some years ago. He said: "there can be no love without suffering, because love always implies renouncement of myself, letting myself go and accepting the other in his otherness; it implies a gift of myself and therefore, emerging from myself."[4]

This is what God has been training us to do from the foundation of the world. It's just that we cannot do it if we're tangled up in sin. Before we can "let ourselves go," we need to have our lives in hand. Before we can give ourselves away, we need to have some possession of ourselves. We need at least some small degree of self-mastery. True love—self-giving love, life-giving love—requires sacrifice, and sacrifice entails suffering.

Whenever people love, this is how they do it. Love is the answer to the riddle of suffering. Suffering is the answer to the riddle of love. Only with Jesus—and specifically with the Paschal Mystery—did God reveal the answer to the perennial riddles of our existence.

In his Passion and in his Pasch, Jesus is leading us, teaching us, and empowering us to live the life of heaven, which is love. His life impels us first to imitate him, then to seek union with him, and finally to let him act in us. Then the Father's will is done. Through the

Paschal Mystery—the hour, the cup—we enter communion with Jesus. We share his life. We participate in it.

Our suffering is his Passion. It is passionate, but not passive in any negative sense. Jesus himself emphasizes that point. He *takes* up his cross and urges us to take up ours. Nobody takes his life. He lays it down. He wants us to do the same, and he gives us the grace to do the same. We grow in this life as we correspond to the grace. We grow through practice, the practice of virtue, yes, but especially the practice of the Paschal sacraments.

WITNESS FOR THE PERSECUTION

The grace and mercy of Christ enable us, in turn, to bear witness, even if only by accepting the "cup" we cannot avoid. For the Eucharist will transform our suffering into sacrifice. It isn't the case that Jesus suffered and died so that we wouldn't have to. It's not a purely substitutionary matter. It's a representative and participatory mystery. He suffered and died in order to endow our sufferings with a redemptive value, something they would never have possessed on their own. He suffered and died in order to invest his love with us. He did this so that our love, while not diminishing our suffering or sparing us from pain, will transform pain into holy passion, suffering into sacrifice. He did this so that our life in Christ might climax in a holy death.

Our death need not be a public spectacle in order to be a Christian witness. Even for the martyrs, the public character of their death was not the essential element. What was essential was the Eucharistic character of their self-giving.[5] As early as A.D. 107 we find Saint Ignatius of Antioch presenting himself as a libation of wine to be poured out in the Roman Colosseum and as wheat to be ground in the teeth of lions.[6] A few years later, Saint Polycarp of Smyrna offers his last words in the form of a Eucharistic prayer, and his burning body gives off not the stench of burning flesh, but the aroma of baking bread and incense.[7]

In extremis, the martyrs take their words from the Eucharistic liturgy. They model their self-offering on Jesus' Eucharistic action. Thus we see the connection not only between Jesus' offering at the seder meal and its consummation on Good Friday—but also between our participation in the Eucharistic cup and our participation in the mystery of holy death. Saint Augustine said it well:

> The martyrs recognized what they ate and drank, so that they could give back the same kind of thing . . . What shall I pay back to the Lord for all the things he has paid back to me?

I will receive the cup of salvation. What is this cup? The bitter but salutary cup of suffering, the cup which the invalid would fear to touch if the doctor did not drink it first. That is what this cup is; we can recognize this cup on the lips of Christ, when he says, *Father, if it can be so, let this cup pass from me.* It is about this cup that the martyrs said, I will receive the cup of salvation and call upon the name of the Lord . . . O, how blessed are those who drank this cup thus! They have finished with suffering and have received honor instead.[8]

Martyrdom is the imitation of Christ, and it's the anticipation of heaven. Jesus' actions in his public ministry were a perfect visible expression of his eternal life with the Father and the Holy Spirit. His is a life of infinite self-giving. He wants us to know that. More, he wants us to live it, with him, as long as we live, which means forever.

But it begins right now. Our Eucharistic life, in the Church, is Paschal, Pentecostal, and Trinitarian. Listen to Saint Paul:

When we cry, "Abba! Father!" it is the Spirit himself bearing witness with our spirit that we are children of God, and if children, then heirs,

heirs of God and fellow heirs with Christ, *provided we suffer with him* in order that we may also be glorified with him. (Romans 8:15–17; emphasis added)

In the Spirit we suffer with the Son as we love the Father. Note that suffering, according to Saint Paul, is not optional.

LAST WORDS

Redemptive suffering is an essential part of our master story. This is what it means for us to bear the image and likeness of God. By the power of the Holy Spirit, our suffering refines our charity, just as our charity transforms our suffering into a living sacrifice that allows God to have his way in our lives.

Even today we sing of our Savior's suffering and his love as synonyms: "Lift high the cross; the love of Christ proclaim." Yet it was not the magnitude of Christ's suffering that saved us but rather the magnitude of his love. Love turned his suffering into an offering at the Last Supper, and that love is the Eucharist. It was the Eucharist that transformed Calvary into a sacrifice rather than merely an execution.

There at the cross Jesus turned death inside out and upside down. Death is the moment we usually associate with the loss of life. But Jesus made it the occasion of giving life. He didn't lose anything at all; he gave his life freely and fully. He transformed it into a gift, a prayer, a sacrifice.

He taught us how to die, and in doing so he taught us how to live. The hour of Jesus' shame and death was not a defeat but rather a victory of life and love over sin and death. And that can be true as well for our own shame, our own sickness, our own sorrow, our own disappointments, our own rejections, and our own death.

Jesus entered the glory of his kingdom at the very moment he manifested the essence of it, which is love to the last, love even in the face of hatred. He had promised: "I tell you I shall not drink again of this fruit of the vine until that day when I drink it new with you in my Father's kingdom" (Matthew 26:29). And he kept his promise.

When did Jesus partake of the fourth cup? At the hour of his death, when his sacrifice was consummated.

When will we? At the hour of our death, when the witness of our life will be consummated.

This entire book is the story of my conversion. I wish I could say my conversion to Jesus was complete when I first encountered him, but that would be untrue.

Conversion is never a one-time event. It's ongoing and ever-deepening. It was for Saint Peter. It was for Saint Paul.

Only at death is our Passover complete, when like Jesus we can truly say, "It is finished."

Notes

CHAPTER 2: PASSOVER AND COVENANT

1. Hayyim Schauss, *The Jewish Festivals: A Guide to Their History and Observance* (New York: Schocken Books, 1996, reprint).

2. On the covenant with Adam, see Gordon P. Hugenberger, *Marriage as a Covenant: Biblical Law and Ethics as Developed from Malachi* (Grand Rapids, MI: Baker Books, 1998); and Scott Hahn, *A Father Who Keeps His Promises: God's Covenant Love in Scripture* (Ann Arbor, MI: Servant, 1998), 37–76.

3. See Josephus, *Jewish War* 2.14.3, 6.9.3.

CHAPTER 3: A TYPICAL SACRIFICE

1. Joshua Berman, *The Temple: Its Symbolism and Meaning Then and Now* (Northvale, NJ: Jason Aronson, 1995), 119.

CHAPTER 4: RITE TURNS

1. *Mishnah Pesachim* 10.5.

CHAPTER 5: THE PASCHAL SHAPE OF THE GOSPELS

1. Raymond Apple, "The Last Supper—A Passover Seder?" *Jerusalem Post,* April 13, 2014, accessed May 27, 2017, from JPost.com.

2. Baruch Bokser, *The Origins of the Seder: The Passover Rite and Early Rabbinic Judaism* (Berkeley: University of California Press, 1984), 25–26.

3. A. Jaubert, *The Date of the Last Supper* (Staten Island, NY: Alba House, 1965).

4. See Eugen Ruckstuhl, *Chronology of the Last Days of Jesus: A Critical Study* (Paris: Desclee, 1965); and James C. VanderKam, *From Revelation to Canon* (Boston: Brill, 2000), 81–127.

5. People sometimes ask why the Church celebrates Holy *Thursday* instead of Tuesday. The short answer is that the feasts days are not, strictly speaking, anniversaries of the events they celebrate. A longer answer would note that the events of the Last Supper have been memorialized on a Tuesday in different times and places in the Church's history.

6. Joachim Jeremias, *The Eucharistic Words of Jesus,* 3rd ed. (London: SCM Press, 1966), 42–61.

7. Pope Benedict XVI, *Sacramentum Caritatis,* 9.

8. Ibid., 10.

CHAPTER 6: BEHOLD THE LAMB

1. *Mishnah Pesahim* 7.1–2.

2. Saint Justin Martyr, *Dialogue with Trypho,* 40.

3. Ibid.

4. Joseph Tabory, "The Crucifixion of the Paschal Lamb," *Jewish Quarterly Review,* January–April 1996, 406.

5. Melito of Sardis, *Peri Pascha,* in Adalbert Hamman, O.F.M., ed., *The Paschal Mystery: Ancient Liturgies and Patristic Texts* (Staten Island, NY: Alba House, 1969), 29.

CHAPTER 7: THE LAMB FROM THE BEGINNING

1. Eugenio Corsini, *The Apocalypse* (Wilmington, DE: Michael Glazier, 1983), 245.

2. See the discussion in Loren L. Johns, *The Lamb Christology of the Apocalypse of John: An Investigation into Its Origins and Rhetorical Force* (Eugene, OR: Wipf and Stock, 2015), 139.

3. Joseph Tabory, "The Crucifixion of the Paschal Lamb," *Jewish Quarterly Review,* January–April 1996, 404.

4. Adalbert Hamman, O.F.M., ed., *The Paschal Mystery: Ancient Liturgies and Patristic Texts* (Staten Island, NY: Alba House, 1969), 32.

5. Melito of Sardis, *Peri Pascha,* translated in Daniel Guernsey, *Adoration* (San Francisco: Ignatius Press, 1999), 35.

6. Philo of Alexandria, *Special Laws* 2.156.

CHAPTER 8: UNLEAVENED BREAD

1. See, for example, Josephus, *Antiquities of the Jews* 17.9.3, 20.5.3, and *Jewish Wars* 2.14.3.

2. Philo, *Special Laws* 2.28.158–160.

CHAPTER 9: THE CUPS

1. David Daube, *The New Testament and Rabbinic Judaism* (Peabody, MA: Hendrickson, 1994 [London, 1956]), 330–332.

2. See W. L. Lane, *The Gospel According to Mark* (Grand Rapids, MI: Eerdmans, 1974), 508: "The cup which Jesus abstained from was the fourth, which ordinarily concluded the Passover fellowship . . . Jesus had used the third cup, associated with the promised work of redemption, to refer to his atoning death . . . The cup which he refused was the cup of consummation."

NOTES

CHAPTER 10: THE HOUR

1. See Raymond E. Brown, *The Death of the Messiah: From Gethsemane to the Grave* (New York: Doubleday, 1994), 2:1007: "In 18:11 Jesus said that he wanted to drink the cup the Father had given him, when Jesus drinks the offered wine, he has finished this commitment made at the beginning of the P[assion] N[arrative]."

2. Saint Augustine of Hippo, *The Harmony of the Gospels* 3.13.

CHAPTER 11: THE CHALICES AND THE CHURCH

1. Saint John Chrysostom, *Instruction to Catechumens* 1.1.

2. Saint Ambrose of Milan, *On the Duties of the Clergy* 2.143.

3. Ibid., 2.138.

4. Saint Optatus of Milevis, *Against the Donatists*, appendix 2.

5. Tertullian, *On Modesty* 10.

6. See Sozomen, *Ecclesiastical History* 2.23, 2.25; Theodoret, *Ecclesiastical History* 2.6; Athanasius, *Apologia Contra Arianos* 2.60, 1.11.

7. Saint Jerome, *Letters* 114.2.

8. See *Didache* 9 and 14.

9. Saint Ignatius of Antioch, *Letter to the Smyrnaeans* 7.

10. Saint Ignatius of Antioch, *Letter to the Ephesians* 1.

11. Saint Ignatius of Antioch, *Letter to the Smyrnaeans* 7.

12. Saint Justin Martyr, *First Apology* 66.

13. See Saint Ignatius of Antioch, *Letter to the Ephesians* 5, *Letter to the Trallians* 7, and *Letter to the Philadelphians* 4.

14. Saint Justin Martyr, *Dialogue with Trypho* 41.

15. *Martyrdom of Polycarp* 14.2. See also L. Goppelt, in G. Kittel and G. Friedrich, eds., *Theological Dictionary of the New Testament*, vol. 6 (Grand Rapids, MI: Eerdmans,

1968), 153: "On the basis of the cup-sayings of Jesus the cup becomes a symbol of martyrdom in early Church writings."

16. Saint Cyprian of Carthage, *Letters* 15.2.

17. Ibid., 53.2.

18. Saint Cyprian of Carthage, *Letters* 55.1.

19. Tertullian, *Scorpiace* 12.

20. Saint Augustine of Hippo, *Exposition on the Psalms* 103.3.

21. Years later, in his 2003 encyclical letter *Ecclesia de Eucharistia,* n. 12, Pope Saint John Paul II would put the matter this way: "The Mass makes present the sacrifice of the Cross; it does not add to that sacrifice nor does it multiply it. What is repeated is its *memorial* celebration, its 'commemorative representation' (*memorialis demonstratio*), which makes Christ's one, definitive redemptive sacrifice always present in time. The sacrificial nature of the Eucharistic mystery cannot therefore be understood as something separate, independent of the Cross or only indirectly referring to the sacrifice of Calvary."

22. The text of the old Baltimore Catechism can be found at many sites on the World Wide Web.

CHAPTER 12: THE PASCHAL SHAPE OF THE LITURGY

1. *Mishnah Pesachim* 10.6.

2. *Mishnah Pesachim* 10.7.

3. Pope Saint John Paul II, *Angelus,* November 30, 1986.

4. Dennis E. Smith, *From Symposium to Eucharist: The Banquet in the Early Christian World* (Minneapolis: Fortress Press, 2003), 32.

5. *Mishnah Pesachim* 10.2–7.

6. Saint Justin Martyr, *First Apology* 65.

7. Saint Irenaeus of Lyons, *Against Heresies* 5.2.3.

8. Saint Irenaeus of Lyons, *Against Heresies* 4.33.2.

9. Saint Cyprian of Carthage, *Letter to Caecilius* 2. This letter is numbered either 62 or 63, depending on the edition.

10. Ibid. Clement of Alexandria also proposes an allegorical interpretation of the action; see *The Instructor* 2.2.

11. Saint Ambrose of Milan, *On the Sacraments* 5.1.4.

12. Edward J. Kilmartin, S.J., *The Eucharist in the Primitive Church* (Englewood, NJ: Prentice-Hall, 1965), 46–47.

CHAPTER 13: THE CHRISTIAN PASSOVER

1. Robert J. Daly, *Christian Sacrifice* (Washington, DC: Catholic University of America Press, 1978), 224.

2. Cheslyn Jones et al., *The Study of Liturgy*, rev. ed. (London: SPCK, 1978), 11.

CHAPTER 14: THE PASCHAL SHAPE OF LIFE

1. Saint Augustine of Hippo, *Exposition on the Psalms* 103.3.

2. Saint Augustine of Hippo, *Sermons on the New Testament* 10.2.

3. Philo of Alexandria, *Questions on the Exodus* 1.11–17.

4. Benedict XVI, visit to Treviso, Italy, July 24, 2007. Retrieved from Zenit.org, June 16, 2017.

5. Cardinal Donald Wuerl develops this idea splendidly in chapter 12 of his book *To the Martyrs* (Steubenville, OH: Emmaus Road, 2015). I discuss it at length in *Letter and Spirit: From Written Text to Living Word in the Liturgy* (New York: Image, 2005), 102–106.

6. Saint Ignatius of Antioch, *Letter to the Romans* 4.

7. *Martyrdom of Polycarp* 14–15.

8. Saint Augustine of Hippo, *Sermons* 329.1–2.

Works Consulted

Berman, Joshua. *The Temple: Its Symbolism and Meaning Then and Now.* Northvale, NJ: Jason Aronson, 1995.

Bokser, Baruch. *The Origins of the Seder: The Passover Rite and Early Rabbinic Judaism.* Berkeley: University of California Press, 1984.

Bouyer, Louis. *Eucharist: Theology and Spirituality of the Eucharistic Prayer.* Notre Dame, IN: University of Notre Dame Press, 1968.

———. *The Paschal Mystery.* London: Allen & Unwin, 1951.

Brown, Raymond E. *The Death of the Messiah: From Gethsemane to the Grave.* New York: Doubleday, 1994.

Cantalamessa, Raniero, O.F.M. Cap. *Easter in the Early Church.* Collegeville, MN: Liturgical Press, 1993.

Corsini, Eugenio. *The Apocalypse.* Wilmington, DE: Michael Glazier, 1983.

Cullmann, Oscar. *Early Christian Worship.* London: SCM Press, 1956.

Cullmann, Oscar, and F. J. Leenhardt. *Essays on the Lord's Supper.* London: Lutterworth Press, 1958.

Daly, Robert J., S.J. *Christian Sacrifice: The Judaeo-Christian Background Before Origen.* Washington, DC: Catholic University of America Press, 1978.

Danielou, Jean, S.J. *The Bible and the Liturgy*. Notre Dame, IN: University of Notre Dame Press, 1956.

———. *From Shadows to Reality: Studies in the Typology of the Fathers*. London: Burns & Oates, 1960.

———. *The Theology of Jewish Christianity*. Chicago: Regnery, 1964.

Daube, David. *The New Testament and Rabbinic Judaism*. London, 1956. Reprint, Peabody, MA: Hendrickson, 1994.

Davila, James R. *Liturgical Works*. Eerdmans Commentaries on the Dead Sea Scrolls, vol. 6. Grand Rapids, MI: Eerdmans, 2000.

de la Taille, Maurice. *The Mystery of Faith*, 2 vols. New York: Sheed & Ward, 1950.

Feeley-Harnick, Gillian. *The Lord's Table: The Meaning of Food in Early Judaism and Christianity*. Washington, DC: Smithsonian Institution Press, 1982.

Hahn, Scott. *Consuming the Word: The New Testament and the Eucharist in the Early Church*. New York: Image, 2013.

———. *A Father Who Keeps His Promises: God's Covenant Love in Scripture*. Ann Arbor, MI: Servant, 1998.

———. *The Lamb's Supper: The Mass as Heaven on Earth*. New York: Doubleday, 1999.

———. *Letter and Spirit: From Written Text to Living Word in the Liturgy*. New York: Doubleday, 2005.

Hahn, Scott, and Kimberly Hahn. *Rome Sweet Home*. San Francisco: Ignatius Press, 1993.

Hamman, Adalbert, O.F.M., ed. *The Paschal Mystery: Ancient Liturgies and Patristic Texts*. Staten Island, NY: Alba House, 1969.

Hugenberger, Gordon P. *Marriage as a Covenant: Biblical Law and Ethics as Developed from Malachi*. Grand Rapids, MI: Baker Books, 1998.

Jeremias, Joachim. *The Eucharistic Words of Jesus*, 3rd ed. London: SCM Press, 1966.

Johns, Loren L. *The Lamb Christology of the Apocalypse of John: An Investigation into Its Origins and Rhetorical Force.* Eugene, OR: Wipf and Stock, 2015.

Jones, Cheslyn, Geoffrey Wainwright, Edward Yarnold, S.J., and Paul Bradshaw, eds. *The Study of Liturgy,* rev. ed. London: SPCK, 1978.

Jungmann, Josef A., S.J. *The Early Liturgy: To the Time of Gregory the Great.* Notre Dame, IN: University of Notre Dame Press, 1959.

———. *The Eucharistic Prayer.* Notre Dame, IN: Fides, 1964.

———. *The Mass of the Roman Rite: Its Origins and Development.* 2 vols. Allen, TX: Christian Classics, 1986.

———. *The Place of Christ in Liturgical Prayer.* London: Geoffrey Chapman, 1965.

Kilmartin, Edward J., S.J. *The Eucharist in the Primitive Church.* Englewood, NJ: Prentice-Hall, 1965.

Kline, Meredith G. *By Oath Consigned: A Reinterpretation of the Covenant Signs of Circumcision and Baptism.* Grand Rapids, MI: Eerdmans, 1968.

Koenig, John. *The Feast of the World's Redemption: Eucharistic Origins and Mission.* Harrisburg, PA: Trinity Press International, 2000.

Lane, W. L. *The Gospel According to Mark.* Grand Rapids, MI: Eerdmans, 1974.

LaPorte, Jean. *The Celebration of the Eucharist: The Origin of the Rite and the Development of Its Interpretation.* Collegeville, MN: Pueblo Books, 1999.

———. *Eucharistia in Philo.* New York: Edwin Mellen, 1983.

Mazza, Enrico. *The Origins of the Eucharistic Prayer.* Collegeville, MN: Pueblo Books, 1995.

Pitre, Brant. *Jesus and the Jewish Roots of the Eucharist: Unlocking the Secrets of the Last Supper.* New York: Doubleday, 2011.

———. *Jesus and the Last Supper.* Grand Rapids, MI: Eerdmans, 2015.

Ratzinger, Joseph Cardinal. *Feast of Faith*. San Francisco: Ignatius Press, 1986.

———. *The Spirit of the Liturgy*. San Francisco: Ignatius Press, 2000.

Sanders, E. P. *Judaism: Practice and Belief 63 BCE–66 CE*. London: SCM Press, 1992.

Sarna, Nahum. *Exploring Exodus: The Heritage of Biblical Israel*. New York: Schocken Books, 1986.

Schauss, Hayyim. *The Jewish Festivals: A Guide to Their History and Observance*. New York: Schocken Books, 1996, reprint.

Skarsaune, Oskar. *In the Shadow of the Temple: Jewish Influences on Early Christianity*. Downers Grove, IL: InterVarsity Press, 2002.

Smith, Dennis E. *From Symposium to Eucharist: The Banquet in the Early Christian World*. Minneapolis: Fortress Press, 2003.

Tabory, Joseph. "The Crucifixion of the Paschal Lamb." *Jewish Quarterly Review,* January–April 1996.

Thurian, Max. *The Eucharistic Memorial*. Richmond, VA: John Knox Press, 1962.

Trocmé, Etienne. *The Passion as Liturgy*. London: SCM Press, 1983.

VanderKam, James C. *From Revelation to Canon*. Boston: Brill, 2000.

Vaux, Roland de, O.P. *Ancient Israel: Its Life and Institutions*. New York: McGraw-Hill, 1965.

Wuerl, Donald. *To the Martyrs*. Steubenville, OH: Emmaus Road, 2015.

Zeitlin, Solomon. "Jesus and the Last Supper." In *The Passover Haggadah*. Edited by Nahum N. Glatzer. New York: Schocken Books, 1989.